OPPOSING VIEWPOINTS® SERIES

Espionage and Intelligence

Other Books of Related Interest

Opposing Viewpoints Series
Digital Rights and Privacy
NATO
Whistleblowers

At Issue Series
Money Laundering
Nuclear Anxiety
Policing in America

Current Controversies Series
America's Role in a Changing World
Cyberterrorism
The Dark Web

> "Congress shall make no law … abridging the freedom of speech, or of the press."
>
> *First Amendment to the U.S. Constitution*

The basic foundation of our democracy is the First Amendment guarantee of freedom of expression. The Opposing Viewpoints series is dedicated to the concept of this basic freedom and the idea that it is more important to practice it than to enshrine it.

Espionage and Intelligence

Avery Elizabeth Hurt, Book Editor

Published in 2025 by Greenhaven Publishing, LLC
2544 Clinton Street,
Buffalo NY 14224

Copyright © 2025 by Greenhaven Publishing, LLC

First Edition

All rights reserved. No part of this book may be reproduced in any form without permission in writing from the publisher, except by a reviewer.

Articles in Greenhaven Publishing anthologies are often edited for length to meet page requirements. In addition, original titles of these works are changed to clearly present the main thesis and to explicitly indicate the author's opinion. Every effort is made to ensure that Greenhaven Publishing accurately reflects the original intent of the authors. Every effort has been made to trace the owners of the copyrighted material.

Cover image: Vector Tradition/Shutterstock.com

Library of Congress CataloginginPublication Data

Names: Hurt, Avery Elizabeth, editor of compilation.
Title: Espionage and intelligence / Avery Elizabeth Hurt, book editor.
Description: First edition. | New York : Greenhaven Publishing, 2024. | Series: Opposing viewpoints | Includes bibliographical references and index. | Audience: Grades 10-12
Identifiers: LCCN 2024001348 | ISBN 9781534509726 (library binding) | ISBN 9781534509719 (paperback)
Subjects: LCSH: Intelligence service. | Espionage.
Classification: LCC JF1525.I6 E874 2024 | DDC 327.12--dc23/eng/20240226
LC record available at https://lccn.loc.gov/2024001348

Manufactured in the United States of America

Website: http://greenhavenpublishing.com

Contents

The Importance of Opposing Viewpoints   11
Introduction   14

Chapter 1: Should Spying Be Abolished?

Chapter Preface   18

1. Espionage at the Dawn of the Nuclear Era   19
   Calder Walton
2. The CIA Dropped the Ball in Ukraine   25
   James Risen and Ken Klippenstein
3. Intelligence Operations Helped Make D-Day a Success   33
   Turner Collins
4. It's Time to Reconsider the Fundamentals of the Intelligence Community   40
   Marvin C. Ott
5. We May Never Know How Many Were Harmed by the CIA's Quest for Mind Control   49
   Terry Gross

Periodical and Internet Sources Bibliography   55

Chapter 2: Should Allies Spy on Each Other?

Chapter Preface   58

1. Five Eyes Nations Surveil Each Other's Citizens   59
   Sumeda Sharma
2. Spying Thrives Under Diplomatic Cover   64
   Eugene Matos and Adrian Zienkiewicz
3. Spying Among Friends Raises Concerns   71
   Daniel Baldino
4. The Need for Security Can Cause Allies to Make Controversial Choices   77
   Amelie Theussen

5. There Are Times When We Must Spy on Our Allies   82
   Elbridge Colby
Periodical and Internet Sources Bibliography   90

Chapter 3: Should the Government Spy on Its Own Citizens?

Chapter Preface   93
1. The NSA Has Made Changes to Spying Programs — but Not Enough   94
   Sarah Childress
2. Yes, Edward Snowden Is a Traitor   101
   Zachary Keck
3. Surveillance Programs Violate the U.S. Constitution   106
   Kevin Reed
4. The FISA Court Invades the Privacy of Americans Without Oversight   113
   Cindy Cohn, Danny O'Brien, and Julian Sanchez
5. After 9/11, Authorities Toe the Line Between Protecting Lives and Protecting Rights   121
   Ryan Lucas
Periodical and Internet Sources Bibliography   128

Chapter 4: Should Corporations Be Allowed to Spy on Private Citizens?

Chapter Preface   131
1. Companies Are Collecting, Analyzing, and Selling Your Data   132
   Anne Toomey McKenna
2. Employee Surveillance Lowers Worker Morale and Should Be Curbed   139
   Evronia Azer
3. Privacy Law Isn't Keeping Up with Technology   144
   Jacqueline Meredith and Peter Holland

4. Watching Workers Is Ethically Questionable and
      Not Always Productive   149
      Linda Rodriguez McRobbie
   5. Most Americans Are Concerned About the Use
      of Their Data   155
      Brooke Auxier and Lee Rainie

Periodical and Internet Sources Bibliography   161

For Further Discussion   163
Organizations to Contact   166
Bibliography of Books   170
Index   172

The Importance of Opposing Viewpoints

Perhaps every generation experiences a period in time in which the populace seems especially polarized, starkly divided on the important issues of the day and gravitating toward the far ends of the political spectrum and away from a consensus-facilitating middle ground. The world that today's students are growing up in and that they will soon enter into as active and engaged citizens is deeply fragmented in just this way. Issues relating to terrorism, immigration, women's rights, minority rights, race relations, health care, taxation, wealth and poverty, the environment, policing, military intervention, the proper role of government—in some ways, perennial issues that are freshly and uniquely urgent and vital with each new generation—are currently roiling the world.

If we are to foster a knowledgeable, responsible, active, and engaged citizenry among today's youth, we must provide them with the intellectual, interpretive, and critical-thinking tools and experience necessary to make sense of the world around them and of the all-important debates and arguments that inform it. After all, the outcome of these debates will in large measure determine the future course, prospects, and outcomes of the world and its peoples, particularly its youth. If they are to become successful members of society and productive and informed citizens, students need to learn how to evaluate the strengths and weaknesses of someone else's arguments, how to sift fact from opinion and fallacy, and how to test the relative merits and validity of their own opinions against the known facts and the best possible available information. The landmark series Opposing Viewpoints has been providing students with just such critical-thinking skills and exposure to the debates surrounding society's most urgent contemporary issues for many years, and it continues to serve this essential role with undiminished commitment, care, and rigor.

The key to the series's success in achieving its goal of sharpening students' critical-thinking and analytic skills resides in its title—

Opposing Viewpoints. In every intriguing, compelling, and engaging volume of this series, readers are presented with the widest possible spectrum of distinct viewpoints, expert opinions, and informed argumentation and commentary, supplied by some of today's leading academics, thinkers, analysts, politicians, policy makers, economists, activists, change agents, and advocates. Every opinion and argument anthologized here is presented objectively and accorded respect. There is no editorializing in any introductory text or in the arrangement and order of the pieces. No piece is included as a "straw man," an easy ideological target for cheap point-scoring. As wide and inclusive a range of viewpoints as possible is offered, with no privileging of one particular political ideology or cultural perspective over another. It is left to each individual reader to evaluate the relative merits of each argument—as he or she sees it, and with the use of ever-growing critical-thinking skills—and grapple with his or her own assumptions, beliefs, and perspectives to determine how convincing or successful any given argument is and how the reader's own stance on the issue may be modified or altered in response to it.

This process is facilitated and supported by volume, chapter, and selection introductions that provide readers with the essential context they need to begin engaging with the spotlighted issues, with the debates surrounding them, and with their own perhaps shifting or nascent opinions on them. In addition, guided reading and discussion questions encourage readers to determine the authors' point of view and purpose, interrogate and analyze the various arguments and their rhetoric and structure, evaluate the arguments' strengths and weaknesses, test their claims against available facts and evidence, judge the validity of the reasoning, and bring into clearer, sharper focus the reader's own beliefs and conclusions and how they may differ from or align with those in the collection or those of their classmates.

Research has shown that reading comprehension skills improve dramatically when students are provided with compelling, intriguing, and relevant "discussable" texts. The subject matter of these collections could not be more compelling, intriguing, or urgently relevant to today's students and the world they are poised to inherit. The anthologized articles and the reading and discussion questions that are included with them also provide the basis for stimulating, lively, and passionate classroom debates. Students who are compelled to anticipate objections to their own argument and identify the flaws in those of an opponent read more carefully, think more critically, and steep themselves in relevant context, facts, and information more thoroughly. In short, using discussable text of the kind provided by every single volume in the Opposing Viewpoints series encourages close reading, facilitates reading comprehension, fosters research, strengthens critical thinking, and greatly enlivens and energizes classroom discussion and participation. The entire learning process is deepened, extended, and strengthened.

For all of these reasons, Opposing Viewpoints continues to be exactly the right resource at exactly the right time—when we most need to provide readers with the critical-thinking tools and skills that will not only serve them well in school but also in their careers and their daily lives as decision-making family members, community members, and citizens. This series encourages respectful engagement with and analysis of opposing viewpoints and fosters a resulting increase in the strength and rigor of one's own opinions and stances. As such, it helps make readers "future ready," and that readiness will pay rich dividends for the readers themselves, for the citizenry, for our society, and for the world at large.

Introduction

> "Can a democracy maintain an effective, capable intelligence service without doing violence to the norms, processes, and institutions of democracy, itself?"
>
> —Marvin C. Ott

Spying is an ancient art. Though the practice certainly goes back much further, espionage is mentioned in the Bible. When Israel is preparing to enter Canaan, Moses sends twelve spies, one from each tribe, to scout the country and gauge the strength of the people living there.

In the United States, the practice of spying goes all the way back to the nation's beginnings, the Revolutionary War. When George Washington became commander of the Continental army, he organized spy rings, used secret codes, analyzed intelligence, and used espionage to deceive the British. Historians think Washington's deft use of the arts of espionage had a major impact on the outcome of the war.

During World War II, intelligence on the part of the United States and the other Allies played a major role in defeating Nazi Germany. However, spying didn't catch the public imagination until the Cold War. When it did, spy books and movies became very popular. Probably the most famous fictional spy is James Bond, the hero of a series of bestselling books and a wildly popular movie franchise that continues to this day. In the 1960s and 1970s, spies came to television, and viewers enjoyed spy dramas such as *The Man From U.N.C.L.E.*, *I Spy*, and *Mission: Impossible*. Comedy got into the act, too, with the TV show *Get Smart,* which was mostly a parody of *The Man From U.N.C.L.E.*

In reality, espionage is quite different from TV and films, both less exciting and—in some ways—perhaps even more exciting. In this volume, we look at some of the issues surrounding espionage that don't generally make it into popular culture. The first chapter poses the question of whether we should have spy agencies at all. The chapter includes viewpoints that argue that spying doesn't always do that much good, and sometimes can do quite a lot of harm. The chapter opens with the stories of spies who sold America's nuclear secrets to the Soviets and ponders both the motives of these individuals and the outcome of their actions. How much harm did those spies really do, in the end? The chapter closes with a viewpoint describing an ill-fated CIA program that attempted mind control.

In most cases, countries spy on their enemies. However, in the second chapter, we learn that they sometimes spy on their allies. On the surface this seems pretty unethical, but the authors in this chapter debate the pros and cons. Spying on friends might be justified in certain circumstances, some of the authors here argue. And, as one author points out in a viewpoint about spying at diplomatic embassies, nations may have good reasons to overlook a little spying among friends.

If spying on friends is questionable, what about spying on your own citizens? In a free society such practices would seem to be completely unacceptable. Yet, the United States government was caught doing just that when documents from the National Security Agency (NSA) were leaked in 2013. This sparked debate about whether or not such spying was justified in the interest of national security. The authors represented in Chapter 3 take up that question, discussing whether or not such practices are constitutional. In addition, they offer opinions about the guilt or innocence of Edward Snowden, the man who brought the NSA's spying to the attention of the public. Was he a traitor? A hero? Or merely a whistleblower, deserving of the protections offered to whistleblowers?

Governments aren't the only entities that spy on citizens. Some of the most in-depth surveillance of individuals is being done by corporations, not to protect the nation's security, but to make money. In Chapter 4, the authors take a look at this chilling practice, looking at both the habit of collecting and selling data and the practice of monitoring workers while they work from home.

Spying in the 21st century is a far different activity than it was when the twelve spies sneaked into Canaan or even when George Washington deployed spies to keep tabs on the British army. The methods and motives are different, of course, but so are the complex ethical questions that have always surrounded the practice of spying. In *Opposing Viewpoints: Espionage and Intelligence* you will get a taste of some of the controversies brought about by espionage in the modern world.

CHAPTER 1

Should Spying Be Abolished?

Chapter Preface

In 1929, U.S. Secretary of State Henry L. Stimson shut down the Black Chamber. This was a U.S. agency intended to break encrypted codes of foreign embassies. Why? Because, Stimson said, "Gentlemen do not read each other's mail." In the years since, all types of people—gentle and not—have spent a great deal of time reading each other's mail. However, recently many experts have argued that the Central Intelligence Agency (CIA)—and in fact the entire U.S. intelligence community—should be disbanded. Their reasons are not so courtly, however. Some critics think intelligence agencies are useless. Some think they are dangerous. In either case, they aren't a wise use of U.S. funds.

Meanwhile, others point to the great successes of U.S. intelligence, such as its role in capturing Osama bin Laden and preventing innumerable terrorist attacks. Some argue that effective national security is not possible without the use of intelligence.

In this chapter, we hear of both missteps and triumphs of U.S. intelligence agencies. These viewpoints highlight both the good and the bad of the intelligence community, or the IC for short. One author details the intelligence failures leading up to Russian president Vladimir Putin's invasion of Ukraine in 2022. Another counters with the story of the successful D-Day invasion that turned things around in World War II. This achievement could not have happened without crafty misdirection on the part of allied intelligence services. Yet another author discusses the difficulties of maintaining effective intelligence agencies and a robust democracy at the same time. Intelligence requires secrecy, and democracy requires openness, this author points out.

The closing viewpoint describes one of the most bizarre operations of the CIA, a mind-control experiment, to highlight the potential dangers of agencies that operate with little oversight. This would not be the first or the last time human rights violations occurred in the name of intelligence.

Viewpoint 1

> "Soviet espionage inside the Manhattan Project would change history. By the end of World War II, Stalin's spies had delivered the secrets of the atomic bomb to the Kremlin."

Espionage at the Dawn of the Nuclear Era

Calder Walton

In this viewpoint, Calder Walton discusses the Manhattan Project, an initiative from World War II that led to the development of the atomic bomb, and J. Robert Oppenheimer's role in this project. As Walton explains, Oppenheimer was frequently suspected of being a Soviet spy, but evidence indicates that despite being targeted by Soviet intelligence multiple times he never partook in spying. However, as this viewpoint explains, other scientists involved in the Manhattan Project did work as Soviet spies, and the secrets uncovered and shared with the Soviets through espionage would have a lasting impact. Calder Walton is assistant director of the Applied History Project and Intelligence Project at Harvard Kennedy School.

"How the Soviets Stole Nuclear Secrets and Targeted Oppenheimer, the 'Father of the Atomic Bomb,'" by Calder Walton, The Conversation, July 24, 2023, https://theconversation.com/how-the-soviets-stole-nuclear-secrets-and-targeted-oppenheimer-the-father-of-the-atomic-bomb-204885. Licensed under CC BY-ND 4.0 International.

As you read, consider the following questions:

1. According to this viewpoint, why was J. Robert Oppenheimer suspected of being a Soviet spy?
2. What motives does Walton offer for scientists in the Manhattan Project who agreed to be Soviet spies?
3. In what ways does Walton say that Soviet nuclear espionage changed history?

"Oppenheimer," the epic new movie directed by Christopher Nolan, takes audiences into the mind and moral decisions of J. Robert Oppenheimer, leader of the team of brilliant scientists in Los Alamos, New Mexico, who built the world's first atomic bomb. It's not a documentary, but it gets the big historical moments and subjects right.

The issues that Nolan depicts are not relics of a distant past. The new world that Oppenheimer helped to create, and the nuclear nightmare he feared, still exists today.

Russian President Vladimir Putin is threatening to use nuclear weapons in his war in Ukraine. Iran is doing everything it can to develop nuclear weapons. China is expanding its nuclear arsenal. Hostile governments like China are stealing U.S. defense technologies, including from Los Alamos.

Charges that Oppenheimer was a Soviet spy and a security risk – a major focus of the movie – have been disproved. In December 2022, the Biden administration posthumously voided the U.S. Atomic Energy Commission's 1954 decision to revoke Oppenheimer's security clearance, calling that process biased and unfair. Declassified records reveal that Soviet spying on the U.S. atomic bomb effort advanced Moscow's bomb program, but Oppenheimer was no spy.

Oppenheimer's Perspective

Oppenheimer joined the Manhattan Project, a nationwide effort to build an atomic bomb before the Nazis developed one, in 1942. The scientists he led at the Los Alamos site were probably the most talented group of minds ever assembled in a single laboratory, including 12 eventual Nobel laureates.

In 1954, at the height of the McCarthy era, Oppenheimer was accused of being a communist and even a Soviet spy. What's the truth?

We know that in the 1930s, and until 1943, Oppenheimer was a Communist sympathizer. His brother Frank and his girlfriend Jean Tatlock belonged to the Communist Party of the United States, and Oppenheimer's wife Katherine was a former member.

For Oppy, as his students called him, Marxism was intellectually interesting, but it was also practical. Oppenheimer saw communism as the best defense against the rise of fascism in Europe, which, being of Jewish heritage, was personal for him.

By 1943, however, Oppenheimer's support for Communist Party causes shifted – evidently, as he realized the enormity of his mission to produce an atomic bomb. That year, Oppenheimer helped U.S. Army security officers identify scientists he believed were communists.

Russian Overtures

Oppenheimer was a top target for Soviet intelligence, which assigned him the code names CHESTER and CHEMIST. He was also being cultivated by Soviet intelligence officers. But being targeted and cultivated for recruitment is not the same as being a recruited spy.

As the movie shows, in 1943, Oppenheimer's academic colleague at the University of California, Berkeley, Haakon Chevalier, told Oppenheimer that a British scientist working in San Francisco could relay information to the Soviets. Oppenheimer rejected the approach, but for reasons that remain unclear, he did not inform authorities for several months.

Over the ensuing years, Oppenheimer provided at least three versions of the story, sometimes involving his brother Frank. It seems likely that Robert was trying to protect his brother from Army security.

Archives made available after the Soviet Union's collapse now establish beyond doubt that Oppenheimer was not a Soviet agent. In fact, Soviet intelligence reports about the Manhattan Project reveal that at key points, Stalin's spy chiefs were frustrated that their operatives had not recruited Oppenheimer. But the Russians did penetrate the Manhattan Project – the greatest security breach in U.S. history.

All the Kremlin's Men

Multiple scientists who worked on the Manhattan Project provided critical information about U.S. atomic bomb research to the Soviet Union.

"Oppenheimer" focuses on Klaus Fuchs, a brilliant theoretical physicist who fled from Nazi Germany to Britain and became a British naturalized subject. From the time he started to work on Britain's wartime atom bomb project, Fuchs was in what he later described as "continuous contact" with Soviet intelligence, providing theoretical calculations that were necessary to build the atom bomb.

General Leslie Groves, the military commander of the Manhattan Project, later blamed the British for failing to identify Fuchs as a Soviet spy. That's correct. But the declassified dossier on Fuchs from Britain's security service, MI5, shows that at the time, the agency did not have any positive, reliable evidence of Fuchs's communism. MI5 knew that Fuchs was anti-Nazi, but not that he was pro-Soviet.

As I discuss in my new book, "Spies: The Epic Intelligence War Between East and West," other spies at Los Alamos included a prodigious scientist, Theodore "Ted" Hall (code name MLAD, or "Young"); Julius Rosenberg (code name ANTENNA, later LIBERAL); David Greenglass (BUMBLEBEE, CALIBER). Other Soviet spies, like the British scientist Alan Nunn May, worked in other parts of the Manhattan Project.

These men had multiple motives for betraying U.S. atomic secrets. They were communist true believers and thought atomic weapons were too powerful to be held by one country alone. Moreover, they had a (misguided) defense – that the Soviet Union was America's wartime ally, so they were "only" delivering secrets to an allied government. But as Nolan correctly shows in the movie, when Chevalier approached Oppenheimer with the same argument, Oppenheimer retorted that it was still treason.

Soviet espionage inside the Manhattan Project would change history. By the end of World War II, Stalin's spies had delivered the secrets of the atomic bomb to the Kremlin. This accelerated Moscow's bomb project. When the Soviets detonated their first atomic weapon in August 1949, it was a replica of the weapon built at Los Alamos and dropped by the Americans on Nagasaki.

Even now, nearly 80 years later, secrets about Soviet nuclear espionage are still emerging. One Soviet agent whose espionage has only recently been revealed is George Koval (code name DEVAL), an American engineer who was drafted into the Manhattan Project, where he worked on polonium bomb "initiators" at a facility in Dayton, Ohio.

After Koval died in 2006, at the age of 93, Russia's ministry of defense disclosed that the initiator for the first Soviet atomic bomb was prepared to specifications provided by Koval. Putin posthumously honored Koval as a "Hero of Russia," offering a champagne toast in his honor.

New Targets

If Nolan's film inspires audiences to read the deeply researched biography of Oppenheimer by Kai Bird and Martin Sherwin, which inspired Nolan to make this movie, or other accounts of the Manhattan Project or the Cold War, they will find that the underlying tissues of science and espionage remain alive.

Today, the world stands at the edge of technological revolutions that will transform societies in the 21st century, much as nuclear weapons did in the 20th century: artificial intelligence, quantum computing and biological engineering. Watching "Oppenheimer" makes me wonder whether hostile foreign governments may already have stolen keys to unlocking these new technologies, in the same way the Soviets did with the atom bomb.

Viewpoint 2

> "The CIA got it completely wrong. They thought Russia would win right away."

The CIA Dropped the Ball in Ukraine

James Risen and Ken Klippenstein

In this viewpoint, we shift to modern times. Here, James Risen and Ken Klippenstein ask why the CIA was wrong to expect that Russian President Vladimir Putin would quickly conquer Ukraine when his forces invaded in 2022. Mistakes like this are why some experts think the CIA is no longer useful or effective. The authors examine that and other failures of the agency in this viewpoint and explain what led to these failures. James Risen is a Pulitzer Prize–winning journalist and author. Ken Klippenstein is an investigative reporter who writes for the Intercept.

As you read, consider the following questions:

1. What were the immediate consequences of the CIA's report to President Biden that Kyiv would fall in a matter of days?
2. How, according to this viewpoint, was this failure similar to the failures of the agency in the 1980s and early 1990s, when the Berlin Wall fell and the Soviet Union collapsed?

"The CIA Thought Putin Would Quickly Conquer Ukraine. Why Did They Get It So Wrong?," by James Risen and Ken Klippenstein, The Intercept, October 5, 2022. Reprinted by permission.

3. What do these authors say is the reason U.S. intelligence failed to spot the depth of corruption in the Russian system?

Ever since Ukraine launched a successful counteroffensive against Russian forces in late August, American officials have tried to claim credit, insisting that U.S. intelligence has been key to Ukraine's battlefield victories.

Yet U.S. officials have simultaneously downplayed their intelligence failures in Ukraine — especially their glaring mistakes at the outset of the war. When Putin invaded in February, U.S. intelligence officials told the White House that Russia would win in a matter of days by quickly overwhelming the Ukrainian army, according to current and former U.S. intelligence officials, who asked not to be named to discuss sensitive information.

The Central Intelligence Agency was so pessimistic about Ukraine's chances that officials told President Joe Biden and other policymakers that the best they could expect was that the remnants of Ukraine's defeated forces would mount an insurgency, a guerrilla war against the Russian occupiers. By the time of the February invasion, the CIA was already planning how to provide covert support for a Ukrainian insurgency following a Russian military victory, the officials said.

U.S. intelligence reports at the time predicted that Kyiv would fall quickly, perhaps in a week or two at the most. The predictions spurred the Biden administration to secretly withdraw some key U.S. intelligence assets from Ukraine, including covert former special operations personnel on contract with the CIA, the current and former officials said. Their account was backed up by a Naval officer and a former Navy SEAL, who were aware of the movements and who also asked not to be named because they were not authorized to speak publicly.

The CIA "got it completely wrong," said one former senior U.S. intelligence official, who is knowledgeable about what the CIA was reporting when the Russian invasion began. "They thought Russia would win right away."

When it became clear that the agency's predictions of a rapid Russian victory had been wrong, the Biden administration sent the clandestine assets that had been pulled out of Ukraine back into the country, the military and intelligence officials said. One U.S. official insisted that the CIA only conducted a partial withdrawal of its assets when the war began, and that the agency "never completely left."

Yet clandestine American operations inside Ukraine are now far more extensive than they were early in the war, when U.S. intelligence officials were fearful that Russia would steamroll over the Ukrainian army. There is a much larger presence of both CIA and U.S. special operations personnel and resources in Ukraine than there were at the time of the Russian invasion in February, several current and former intelligence officials told The Intercept.

Secret U.S. operations inside Ukraine are being conducted under a presidential covert action finding, current and former officials said. The finding indicates that the president has quietly notified certain congressional leaders about the administration's decision to conduct a broad program of clandestine operations inside the country. One former special forces officer said that Biden amended a preexisting finding, originally approved during the Obama administration, that was designed to counter malign foreign influence activities. A former CIA officer told The Intercept that Biden's use of the preexisting finding has frustrated some intelligence officials, who believe that U.S. involvement in the Ukraine conflict differs so much from the spirit of the finding that it should merit a new one. A CIA spokesperson declined to comment about whether there is a presidential covert action finding for operations in Ukraine.

The U.S. intelligence community's stunning failure at the beginning of the war to recognize the fundamental weaknesses in the Russian system mirrors its blindness to the military and economic weaknesses of the Soviet Union in the 1980s, when

Washington failed to predict the fall of the Berlin Wall in 1989 and the collapse of the Soviet Union in 1991. While not all U.S. intelligence analysts underestimated the Ukrainian will to fight, the community's missteps in Ukraine came just months after American intelligence gravely underestimated how fast the U.S.-backed government in Afghanistan would collapse in 2021, leading to a rapid takeover by the Taliban.

Some senior U.S. intelligence officials have since admitted they were wrong in projecting a quick Russian victory. In March, Avril

The CIA's Hunt for Bin Laden Damaged Public Health Campaigns in Pakistan

AUDIE CORNISH: It took the U.S. nearly a decade to track down Osama bin Laden following his role in the 9/11 attacks. And the effort to locate him ended up having unexpected and long-term consequences for public health campaigns in Pakistan. NPR's Jackie Northam reports from Islamabad.

JACKIE NORTHAM: In early 2011, U.S. intelligence hunting for Osama bin Laden had honed in on a compound in the town of Abbottabad in eastern Pakistan. But they wanted to make sure it was the right place, so the CIA employed a Pakistani doctor, Shakil Afridi, to organize a hepatitis B vaccination program. The idea was to vaccinate the children living in the compound, then test the DNA on the used syringes to see if they were related to bin Laden. The doctor went to the door but wasn't allowed in. Instead, Afridi was given a phone number to try again later. That phone was ultimately linked to bin Laden. A few months later, Navy SEALs stormed the compound.

NAAZIR MAHMOOD: I remember the day very well. In the morning, I think around 11 o'clock, I switched on the TV. And the news was there that Osama bin has been killed in Abbottabad.

Haines, the director of national intelligence, acknowledged during a Senate Intelligence Committee hearing that the CIA didn't do well "in terms of predicting the military challenges that [Putin] has encountered with his own military."

The director of the Defense Intelligence Agency, Army Lt. Gen. Scott Berrier, said at the same March hearing that "my view was that, based on a variety of factors, that the Ukrainians were not as ready as I thought they should be, therefore I questioned their will to fight, [and] that was a bad assessment on my part."

> NORTHAM: That's Dr. Naazir Mahmood, a Pakistani consultant to international aid groups. He says the government here was furious and embarrassed about the killing of bin Laden on Pakistani soil. It discovered the connection with Afridi, who was arrested and is serving a 23-year sentence. Afridi maintains he never knew he was working for the CIA.
>
> NORTHAM: The repercussions for non-governmental organizations, NGOs, working in Pakistan were profound. Several international aid groups were kicked out of the country . . . , says Aftab Alam Khan, a consultant for international development organizations.
>
> AFTAB ALAM KHAN: There was already some kind of deficit of trust with the NGOs and civil society organizations. But that incident basically magnified and amplified the problems. And we are now in a situation where the NGOs are regulated in a very tough manner.
>
> NORTHAM: … The raid also affected ongoing vaccination campaigns, like a polio eradication effort. Many religious leaders warned the CIA was involved in that campaign as well. The number of people refusing the polio vaccination spiked, and health workers were targeted. Even now, Khan says there's still an air of suspicion that lingers from the bin Laden raid.
>
> "How The CIA's Hunt for Bin Laden Impacted Public Health Campaigns In Pakistan," by Jackie Northam, National Public Radio Inc. (NPR), September 6, 2021.

"I think assessing … morale, and a will to fight is a very difficult analytical task," he added. "We had different inputs from different organizations. And at least from my perspective as director, I did not do as well as I could have."

Yet these admissions mask a more fundamental failure that officials have not fully acknowledged: U.S. intelligence did not recognize the significance of rampant corruption and incompetence in the Putin regime, particularly in both the Russian army and Moscow's defense industries, the current and former intelligence officials said. U.S. intelligence missed the impact of corrupt insider dealing and deceit among Putin loyalists in Moscow's defense establishment, which has left the Russian army a brittle and hollow shell.

"There was no reporting on the corruption in the Russian system," said the former senior intelligence official. "They missed it, and ignored any evidence of it."

Following a string of Russian defeats, even prominent Russian analysts have begun to openly blame the corruption and deceit that plagues the Russian system. On Russian television last weekend, Andrey Gurulyov, the former deputy commander of Russia's southern military district and now a member of the Russian Duma, blamed his country's losses on a system of lies, "top to bottom."

Additionally, Putin imposed an invasion plan on the Russian military that was impossible to achieve, one current U.S. official argued. "You can't really separate out the issue of Russian military competency from the fact that they were shackled to an impossible plan, which led to poor military preparation," the official said.

After Russia's defeat in Lyman, in eastern Ukraine, last weekend, retired Army Lt. Gen. Ben Hodges, who commanded U.S. Army forces in Europe from 2014 until 2018, also admitted that he had "overestimated Russia's capabilities" before it invaded Ukraine because he "failed to realize the depth of corruption" in the Russian Ministry of Defense.

The inability of the U.S. intelligence community to recognize the significance of Russian corruption appears to be the result of an over-reliance on technical intelligence. Before the war, high-tech satellites and surveillance systems allowed the U.S. to track the deployment of Russian troops, tanks, and planes, and to eavesdrop on Russian military officials, enabling U.S. intelligence to accurately predict the timing of the invasion. But it would have needed more human spies inside Russia to see that the Russian army and defense industries were deeply corrupt.

Since the war began, a long list of weaknesses in the Russian military and its defense industries have been exposed, symbolized by the so-called jack-in-the-box flaw in Russian tanks. Ukrainian forces quickly learned that one well-placed shot could blow off a Russian tank turret, sending it sky high and killing the entire crew. It became clear that Russian tanks had been designed and built cheaply — with ammunition stored openly in a ring inside the turret that can explode when the turret is hit — and that crew safety had not been prioritized. In July, Adm. Tony Radakin, Britain's military chief, said that Russia had lost almost 1,700 tanks in Ukraine.

Weak leadership, poor training, and low morale have led to huge casualties among Russian rank and file soldiers. In August, the Pentagon estimated that 70,000 to 80,000 Russian troops had been killed or wounded in Ukraine. Ukraine has also suffered huge casualties, but Russian front-line strength has been badly weakened.

Meanwhile, one of the biggest mysteries for U.S. analysts has been Russia's failure to gain control of Ukraine's skies, despite having a far larger air force. Aircraft design flaws, poor pilot training, and gaps in aircraft maintenance have left Russian aircraft vulnerable to Ukraine's air defenses, which have been bolstered with Stinger missiles and other Western air defense systems.

The failure of U.S. intelligence to see the dysfunction in the Russian army and defense industries means that it also didn't foresee Russia's ongoing battlefield defeats, which are now having a profound political and social impact on both Putin and Russia.

Espionage and Intelligence

Putin has ordered a partial mobilization to replace heavy battlefield losses, sparking large-scale protests. At least 200,000 people have already fled Russia, including thousands of young men seeking to avoid conscription.

VIEWPOINT 3

> "Even the well-regarded Field Marshal known for his cunning found himself duped by the Allies."

Intelligence Operations Helped Make D-Day a Success
Turner Collins

This viewpoint by Turner Collins looks back in history to a time when intelligence operations got it right. The D-Day invasion of Normandy marked a major turning point in the battle against the Nazis and their allies in World War II. In this viewpoint the author tells the story of preparations for the invasion, and how intelligence agencies — both British and American — played a significant role in misleading the German military. This is just one example of the important role intelligence can play in military operations. Turner Collins is a Canadian writer focused on history.

As you read, consider the following questions:

1. What was Operation Overlord?
2. Why was Operation Overlord so important?
3. What was the role of intelligence in ensuring the success of the D-Day invasion?

"Operation Overlord: The Planning & Preparation That Led up to D-Day," by Turner Collins, The Collector, September 4, 2022. Reprinted by permission

Of all the great military battles throughout human history, it is hardly a stretch to say that one of the most famous of these is Operation Overlord, more commonly known as D-day. On June 6th, 1944, the western Allied forces launched the largest amphibious invasion in history: over 350,000 naval, airforce, and army personnel from twelve countries deployed to France's northern coast to establish a new front line against the Germans. This was a herculean effort that required untold amounts of planning, preparation, and coordination, all of which helped drastically shift the focus of the Nazis away from the war with the Soviet Union in the east and forced them to split their attention to multiple fronts. Regardless of doubts about the war there might have been before the summer of 1944, D-day marked a clear and distinct shift in public opinion of the war, proving that victory was undoubtedly and assuredly within reach for the first time in years.

Operation Overlord: Preparation For the D-Day Landings

By the summer of 1944, World War II had been raging across the globe for five years. War had come to Western Europe in the Summer of 1940 when, after the invasion of Poland, the German forces turned their sights on France and Britain. Both had turned down offers of peace from Hitler, who wished to focus his attention on his main enemy, the Soviet Union, and believed that the western Allies had no stomach for war. Through a rapid invasion known as the Battle of France, the Germans completely ejected the Allies from the continent, subjugating France under a collaborationist government and forcing the remnants of the French and British militaries to flee to England. With this, the war in Western Europe had ended on land. However, attempts by Germany to break the resolve of the British would continue through to the Battle of Britain, where Royal Air Force pilots engaged with the members of the Luftwaffe in the skies over England.

During this time, the war raged in the east as millions of Russian and German soldiers clashed across a massive front. Desperate for any help they could get, the Soviets constantly demanded that the Western allies, at first consisting only of the British Empire and its few remaining allies, but later including America, open another front. Despite the war being waged in North Africa and later Italy, the Soviets insisted that this was not enough and that another front was required. Finally, in late 1943, the British and Americans agreed that the Western Allies would open a second major front in France to split and encircle Germany's forces. It was at this point that Operation Overlord was conceived: with one of the most massive mobilizations and concentrations of manpower to be sent in an amphibious landing.

The Details of D-Day

Even though the actual operation had only been planned in the closing months of 1943, a major amphibious invasion of Europe had been in the works for some time. As far back as 1942, the Allies had been working with naval landings in Africa and elsewhere.

One of the major stepping stones in the tactical evolution was known as the Dieppe Raid, an attempt by Commonwealth forces, namely Canadians, in August of 1942 to temporarily seize the port city of Dieppe in northern France. Despite outnumbering the German defenders by a great deal, the Allies' inexperience in landing operations became evident, and the entire operation resulted in a costly defeat. Over half of the landing force was either killed, wounded, or captured, and virtually none of the objectives had been claimed.

Although the landing ended in failure, a great amount of operational information had been gained, essentially providing a "what not to do" playbook for all future landings. One of the more important lessons was that attacks on heavily-defended port cities were unfeasible at best. This would ultimately decide the final location of the D-day landings and result in the Allies constructing massive, hastily-built temporary ports in the wake of the landings.

By the summer of 1944, the Allies were well experienced with naval landings across North Africa, Italy, and the Pacific, which could all be applied to Operation Overlord. Most importantly, a significant amount of preparation and intelligence work went into the landings. It was almost impossible to hide the massing of troops across England from the Germans. However, ever the masters of deception warfare, the British were able to mislead the Germans as to where precisely the invasion would take place. Countless possible locations for the landing were leaked and prepared across Europe in a broad string of deception operations known collectively as Operation Bodyguard. In addition, leading up to the invasion itself, several radar installations along the French coast were destroyed, further blinding the German defenders to the exact nature of the upcoming assault.

German Preparations

The Germans were not idle either. As early as 1942, Hitler had become acutely aware of the possibility of naval incursions into Europe after several raids along the coast, including Dieppe. As a result, a massive chain of fortifications and garrisons were established, intending to create a mighty Atlantic Wall from the border of Spain all the way to the northern tip of Norway. Millions of mines were placed, and tens of thousands of bunkers were built and garrisoned by hundreds of thousands of soldiers, with even more conscripted civilians being used as forced laborers.

Initially, the creation had been slow and sporadic, but the appointment of the fabled General Field Marshal Erwin Rommel, "The Desert Fox" of the African campaigns, would change the dynamic of command. There was a good deal of disagreement within the German high command on how best to respond to an invasion of mainland Europe, and Hitler, who had been at odds with the more experienced Rommel, had seen fit to keep him mainly as a figurehead, rather than giving him an actual command in France or elsewhere.

Even the well-regarded Field Marshal known for his cunning found himself duped by the Allies. Rommel, along with much of the rest of the German Command, firmly believed that the landings would occur at Calais. Despite this, a huge amount of effort and organization was put into securing the fortifications along the Atlantic Wall, even as more troops and valuable war material were shifted to the Eastern Front, where the war with the Soviets was reaching an ever more desperate and bloody struggle.

Because of this, many sections of the wall were left understaffed by what would be considered "second-rate" troops, comprised of older individuals, enlisted POWs, and ex-pats from the East. This was compounded by the command structure, which left command of the critically important and valuable German panzer-divisions split between three individuals: Rommel, Leo Geyr von Schweppenburg, and Hitler himself.

Rommel believed that an invasion must be fought off close to the beaches to mitigate the Allied air superiority he had witnessed in North Africa. In contrast, Geyr von Schweppenburg and other members of the German high command believed that allowing the Allies to land and advance deeper into France and thus out of the range of their naval support would allow for better results with their tank divisions. This lack of coordination and Hitler's insistence on involving himself would ultimately decide the German response on June 6th, 1944.

June 6th, 1944: D-Day

While the term "D-day" in the military simply refers to the day on which an operation or attack is to take place, it would become synonymous with the Normandy landings on the morning of the 6th of June, 1944 and is often remembered even now as "The day of days."

It was originally believed that weather conditions would stall the invasion for some weeks. Even some of the German high command, including Rommel himself, would initially be away from northern France, thinking that the weather would not be calm enough for a landing. Despite this, Allied meteorologists were able to better predict the weather due to complete control over the Atlantic and expected that conditions would be acceptable for the 6th of June.

The first wave over the English Channel would, in fact, not be from the sea but the air, as tens of thousands of paratroopers were deployed throughout the Norman countryside in order to secure critical infrastructure and points ahead of the invasion itself. By dawn, almost 7,000 vessels had made the journey from England and spread out to land some 150,000 soldiers across the coastline of Normandy.'

The major landings were concentrated on five beachheads. Utah and Omaha, the two western-most beaches, were to be stormed by the Americans. Further east was Gold and Juno, assigned to the British and Canadians, respectively. Finally, the eastern-most beach was Sword, assaulted by combined British and free French forces.

Many lessons had been learned from the failure at Dieppe, and excessive preparation had been taken to avoid a repeat. One of the developments was a specialist type of amphibious tank, known as a DD (Duplex Drive) tank, which could propel itself through the water using a waterproof skirt and propellers connected to the main drive. While innovative, these tanks were difficult to operate and not terribly buoyant. This was worsened by the fact that the height of the waves on D-day in some parts of the landings was about six times that for which the DD tanks had previously been tested.

Despite the obstacles, the Allied forces and their new amphibious armor were able to reach the beaches, with the exception of Omaha, where not a single tank was able to make the crossing. Even as the invasion came fully underway, the German high command could not believe this was anything more than a diversion for the real invasion at Pas-de-Calais.

Worse still for the German defenders was the fact that four out of their ten reserve tank regiments required Hitler's personal permission to deploy, and when the landings occurred at roughly 6 am, Hitler was still asleep. The fear of angering Hitler, as is often the case in despotic hierarchies, meant that he was left to rise on his own, some four hours after the initial invasion, before being made aware of what was happening, meaning that some of his most key reserves were unable to act.

Despite the success of the landings across all the beaches, the Allies found their progress significantly slowed, with none of the desired day-one objectives achieved in the face of fierce resistance and bad weather. At this point, the second phase of the Battle of Normandy began as Allied troops attempted to press inwards toward Caen and break out of the beachhead they had created.

VIEWPOINT 4

> "Can a democracy maintain an effective, capable intelligence service without doing violence to the norms, processes, and institutions of democracy, itself?"

It's Time to Reconsider the Fundamentals of the Intelligence Community

Marvin C. Ott

World War II is long over, but the world is once again filled with perils and geopolitical tensions. In this excerpted viewpoint, Marvin Ott looks at the tensions between Congress, which is based on democracy and the free-flow of information, and the intelligence community, which depends on secrecy and top-down control. Since the 9/11 attacks in 2001, the CIA has taken on a larger and—at times—controversial role, and in recent years some have questioned whether the CIA should be exempt from the rule of law that is inherent to protecting the rights of Americans. Marvin Ott is a senior fellow at the Foreign Policy Research Institute.

As you read, consider the following questions:

1. How are threats to U.S. security different now than they were in previous decades?

"Intelligence Oversight in Congress: Perilous Times," by Marvin C. Ott, The Foreign Policy Research Institute, April 17, 2019. Reprinted by permission.

2. What, according to this viewpoint, is the relationship between Congress and the intelligence community (IC) and why it that relationship so difficult?
3. Does Ott think that Congress can effectively oversee the intelligence community? If so, how?

In an ever more complex, interconnected, and dangerous world, the value of high quality intelligence data and analysis for policymakers would seem obvious. The threats to U.S. security are implacable and multifaceted, including cyberattacks, hypersonic weapons, climate change, terrorist networks, and the theft of critical technologies—everything from North Korean nuclear/missile capabilities to Chinese penetration of European digital infrastructure. Understanding the scope and precise nature of these and other threats requires information and insight of a very high order—and some of that will depend on acquiring the secrets of other international actors.

During the Cold War, most of American intelligence collection and analysis focused, understandably, on the Soviet Union. In the late 1990s and particularly after the 9/11 attacks, the focus shifted to international jihadist/terrorist networks and their state supporters. With the U.S. invasion and occupation of both Afghanistan and Iraq (and to a limited extent, Syria), a major effort went into mapping the immediate threats to American forces. In these military theaters, CIA activities often evolved beyond traditional espionage and analysis to commando-type combat roles—essentially indistinguishable from military Special Forces.[1]

The 9/11 attacks and the U.S. response thrust the CIA into key, highly controversial roles—including "special renditions" of Al Qaeda suspects and the use of "enhanced interrogation" methods at CIA-maintained "black sites." It is not possible to conduct such multifaceted, high-risk missions without incurring controversy and criticism. The analysis supporting counterterrorism operations earned its own share of criticism. The failure to "connect the dots" prior to 9/11, misjudgments concerning Iraq's alleged WMD capabilities, and controversial intelligence assessments regarding Iran's alleged nuclear ambitions all provided ample grist for critics. However, none of this produced any serious moves to curtail or reduce U.S. investments in the agencies and programs collectively referred to as the Intelligence Community (IC). On the contrary, intelligence personnel and budgets have been on a rocket ride upward for years. Today, the IC is a multidimensional behemoth comprising civil, military, scientific, space, paramilitary, and analytical components. U.S. "collection" capabilities run the gamut from traditional spy craft through myriad space-based platforms to a variety of ultra-sophisticated electronic/cyber technologies. America's current annual intelligence budget (excluding tactical battlefield intelligence) is estimated at $60 billion—and counting.

Throughout the 72 years since the CIA was established, the primary "customers" for intelligence product have been found at the senior levels of the Executive Branch—and most particularly, in the White House. The "Presidential Daily Brief" (PDB) has long been the gold coin-of-the-realm. A succession of CIA Directors, and more recently Directors of National Intelligence, has jealously guarded the personal access to the president provided by the opportunity to conduct the PDB. When a CIA Director, like George Tenet, could create a close personal bond with the president (built on a shared love of basketball) that is as good as it gets in terms of IC influence and perceived value.

In practice, Congress has long occupied an ambivalent, and secondary, place as a "customer." As a coequal branch of government and the source of IC funding, Congress had an incontestable claim to intelligence product—both as written reports and committee testimony and briefings. This did not prevent many, if not most, in the IC from viewing congressional demands for access to intelligence as unwelcome and even, somehow, illegitimate. Distrust of the Congress runs deep in the intelligence agencies—the assumptions being that Congress can never fully appreciate what intelligence professionals do, that Congress is unable to keep secrets, that congressional members and staff are looking for information that they can misuse for political purposes, and simply that Congress is just "not one of us."

These attitudes highlight the fundamental difficulties in creating and conducting effective congressional oversight of the IC. But the difficulties go deeper than attitudes; there is a fundamental tension between the processes and values that animate political democracy and those of the cloistered world of intelligence. Consider the contrasts. Democracy requires an informed electorate and the relatively free flow of information. Intelligence agencies operate according to entirely different principles: secrecy, need-to-know, and compartmentation of classified information. Democracies are typically suspicious of concentrated power and tend to devolve significant authority downward and outward toward provincial/state and municipal authorities. Intelligence agencies, however, concentrate and centralize both authority and access to information. Democracies are rooted in the rule of law and that law in turn is based on broadly held values in the society. Intelligence, by contrast, often requires special exemptions under domestic law and regularly involves violating the laws of other countries. In most countries and at most times, intelligence has been practiced as a ruthless business that in the end recognizes only the law of success and survival with one measure of merit: did it work? Although not specifically enshrined in the Constitution, privacy has assumed the status over time as a basic right of citizens. However, when an individual becomes an employee of the CIA, he or she largely forfeits such rights vis-à-vis the IC. A condition of employment is a "full scope" polygraph designed to probe and lay bare the most private behavior and motivations. Finally, democracy at some fundamental level requires a degree of mutual trust among citizens and between citizens and government. Within the intelligence world, the price of security is vigilance and with vigilance comes an ingrained suspicion concerning the motives and activities of coworkers and counterparts.

All this adds up to a dilemma. Can a democracy maintain an effective, capable intelligence service without doing violence to the norms, processes, and institutions of democracy, itself? Furthermore, can an elected legislature effectively oversee and manage a modern, capable, intelligence apparatus? The problem is particularly acute in parliamentary systems where the fusing of legislature and executive creates a fundamental structural impediment to independent legislative oversight. For the U.S., however, with its almost unique separation of powers, legislative oversight is feasible—at least in principle.[2]

Feasible does not mean workable. There are obvious and difficult questions whether a highly politicized institution (Congress) dedicated to free debate and wide-open public access could ever be a reliable custodian of the nation's most sensitive secrets—much less serve as an effective overseer and critic.

It is worth noting that congressional oversight is particularly important in the case of intelligence given the clandestine nature of the enterprise. The press and other myriad watchdog organizations cannot provide the kind of public scrutiny of the IC that they can for, say the Department of Energy or the State Department.

A detailed review of the tortured history of congressional oversight of intelligence is beyond the scope of this essay. Suffice to say, that history began with an extended, initial period (1947 through the 1970s) of relaxed old-boy understandings between senior members of the Senate, notably Richard Russell (D-GA), and various CIA Directors. In that era, Congress asked few questions and Directors volunteered little—except their budget requirements. However, by the late 1970s, the landscape that sustained that clubby world had changed dramatically. The catalysts came in the form of a series of high profile controversies including a Vietnam War CIA operation using targeted assassinations (Phoenix Program), the CIA role in Chile and the death of President Allende, and the broader rending of the political fabric occasioned by the Vietnam War and the Watergate scandal. All this led Congress, for the first time, to get serious about congressional oversight of the CIA and other secret programs. Two special purpose vehicles, the Church Committee (Senate) and the Pike Committee (House) produced legislation creating two new oversight Committees: the Senate Select Committee on Intelligence (SSCI)[3] and the House Permanent Select Committee on Intelligence (HPSCI). The Committees were empowered by their authorizing statutes to obtain any necessary information from the intelligence agencies, including the most sensitive and closely held secrets. As a practical matter, both committees agreed to avoid asking for the identity of specific agents and to stay away from liaison relationships that the CIA had with other foreign intelligence entities.

It was one thing to establish committees; it was quite another to figure out how to operate them effectively. Among the intelligence agencies, the initial inclination, understandably, was to see this new congressional initiative as unwelcome and even threatening. Everyone knew that, despite the formal authorities of the select committees, there were myriad ways the IC could frustrate oversight—through obfuscation, concealment, delay, and even deception. The SSCI, for example, had a staff of about thirty. They were tasked with overseeing an IC where just the three most important agencies (CIA, NSA, and DIA) had tens of thousands of employees and controlled trillions of pieces of discrete data. The committee staff could not possibly be productive without a degree of cooperation on the part of the agencies. But such cooperation had to be earned. After an initial two- or three-year period of "getting to know you," the SSCI and the IC—perhaps against the odds—settled into a productive working relationship.

[…]

A productive relationship between congressional oversight and the IC is by its very nature, tenuous and fragile. And, in fact, as the tenure of Sen. Boren and Sen. Cohen on the SSCI came to an end (1989-91), the effectiveness of the committee rapidly eroded. Under a succession of Chairmen D. DeConcini (D-AZ), A. Specter (R-PA), and R. Shelby (R/AL), all the safeguards built by Boren and Cohen fell away. The committee staff was hired with political loyalty and service, not professional competence, in mind. Members of the committee arrayed themselves as political partisans (with majority and minority staffs) producing a deeply divided (and often paralyzed) committee as a result. Chairmen showed an increasing proclivity to use intelligence products as weapons in their various political battles. Sen. Shelby conducted a long-running (and utterly pointless) personal feud with CIA Director George Tenet.

[…]

When Sen. D. Feinstein (D-CA) assumed the leadership of the SSCI in 2009, she inherited a broken institution. Her efforts to rebuild the committee were derailed as she became mired in a bitter, long-running, struggle with the CIA over the issue of whether its interrogation of some 9/11 suspects amounted to "torture" (including waterboarding). The ultimate result was condemnatory SSCI report, endorsed by Democrats and rejected by Republicans that left the CIA in a defensive crouch trying to protect its operatives against possible criminal prosecution. The net result was poisonous for both the SSCI and the CIA.

In 2015, Sen. R. Burr (R-NC) became chairman of the SSCI and two years later Sen. M. Warner (D-VA) joined him as Ranking Minority Member. They have made the first sustained effort in over 25 years to rebuild the SSCI on a non-(or less) partisan, more professional basis. The HPSCI, however, went in a very different direction. It became deeply divided along partisan political lines with the majority led by Chairman D. Nunes (R-CA) who saw his (and the committee's) role as defending President Trump irrespective of fact or merit. The minority was led by Rep. A. Schiff (D-CA) who positioned the Democrats as critics of Trump and Nunes, particularly concerning Russian attempts to manipulate the 2016 election. The 2018 congressional elections flipped the roles of Nunes and Schiff, and now the Democrats have focused the oversight efforts of the HPSCI on the White House and Russia.

The election of Donald Trump as President in 2016 has completely upended the established relationship between the IC and the White House/Executive Branch. It began immediately after the inauguration when the newly elected president used CIA sacred ground (where fallen agents are memorialized) for a political rant replete with factual falsehoods. It quickly became evident that Mr. Trump had neither the patience nor the interest to read IC product. He could barely sit still for even the most summary oral briefing. The president's statements and actions repeatedly demonstrated that he was getting most of his "intelligence" from hours of watching Fox network entertainment programming.

If there was ever any doubt concerning Mr. Trump's disregard, even hostility, regarding the work of the intelligence agencies, it was dispelled when the leadership of the IC testified before Congress in late January. That testimony graphically underlined differences between the intelligence professionals and the president concerning such high profile issues as North Korean nuclear/missile programs, the "defeat" of ISIS, and Iran's compliance with its nuclear treaty obligations. Mr. Trump reacted by publicly rejecting their conclusions, berating their performance and declaring the IC leadership "needs to go back to school."

The assault on the IC has not been confined to the White House. The Attorney General, William Barr, while recently testifying before a Senate subcommittee, volunteered the startling observation that the Trump campaign had been the victim of "spying" by intelligence agencies—perhaps with "predicate," perhaps not. This gratuitous attack left the AG sounding like a conspiracy maven on the dark web. In fact, the "predicate" for the FBI investigation of possible Russian involvement with the Trump campaign has long been on the public record in fulsome detail.

For the IC, all this is a dramatic—and traumatic—turn of events. When Sean Hannity has far more influence on the president's worldview than the DNI, we have crossed into an incomprehensible twilight zone. At the same time, the congressional oversight committees (and others) have emerged as receptive, sympathetic consumers of intelligence—eliciting information and analysis that the White House does not want to hear.

[…]

At a minimum, we seem to have reached a point where the long-established verities surrounding the IC, as well as its congressional overseers, are in question. The IC can—for a time—pretend that nothing has changed. But, in fact, everything has changed. Consequently, it is time to reconsider the fundamentals, including the relationship between the Intelligence Community, the Congress, and the broader public.

Notes

[1] CIA paramilitary operations are well documented. The first U.S. forces into Afghanistan after the 9/11 attacks were CIA commandos, not military Special Forces—much to the irritation of the Secretary of Defense, Donald Rumsfeld. CIA paramilitaries have routinely manned outposts along the Afghanistan/Pakistan border jointly with Special Forces. The current CIA website offers career opportunities as "Paramilitary Operations/Special Skills officer" with a starting salary up $103,639 or higher, plus a "one-time hiring bonus of up to 21 percent of base pay."

[2] Paradoxically, perhaps, the Constitutional separation of powers enables congressional oversight providing Congress with independent authority as a coequal branch of government—fully empowered to examine and judge Executive policies and actions. The capacity to act on those judgments ultimately rests on the power of the purse—to provide or withhold funding. For example, by law, the CIA must brief "covert actions" to the Intelligence Committees in advance of their final approval by the President. If the Committees express strong reservations, those programs are almost always aborted or greatly modified. In the extreme case, Congress can withhold funding.

[3] This analysis focuses on the SSCI because the writer served as Deputy Staff Director of that Committee and can therefore discuss it with greater familiarity. In addition, the SSCI, under Boren and Cohen, was clearly more consequential than the HPSCI. All of the authorizing language that became law during that period came from the SSCI.

VIEWPOINT 5

> *"The top-secret nature of Gottlieb's work makes it impossible to measure the human cost of his experiments."*

We May Never Know How Many Were Harmed by the CIA's Quest for Mind Control

Terry Gross

In this viewpoint, Terry Gross describes a very strange program of the CIA called MK-ULTRA, which existed from the 1950s to the early 1960s. According to this viewpoint, which discusses an interview with journalist Stephen Kinzer, this attempt to develop mind-control tools was not only unsupervised by the U.S. government, but unknown to most other agencies and officials. The damage done to innumerable people shows the dangers of providing limited oversight to intelligence agencies like the CIA. Terry Gross is a journalist and host of NPR's "Fresh Air."

As you read, consider the following questions:

1. Why was the CIA interested in mind control?
2. Who was Sidney Gottlieb?
3. Why do we know so little about this program even today?

©2019 National Public Radio, Inc. NPR news report titled "The CIA's Secret Quest For Mind Control: Torture, LSD And A 'Poisoner In Chief'" by Terry Gross and Stephen Kinzer was originally published on npr.org on September 9, 2019, and is used with the permission of NPR. This interview by Stephen Kinzer was broadcast in 2019 on Fresh Air with Terry Gross, which is produced by WHYY in Philadelphia and distributed by NPR. Any unauthorized duplication is strictly prohibited.

During the early period of the Cold War, the CIA became convinced that communists had discovered a drug or technique that would allow them to control human minds. In response, the CIA began its own secret program, called MK-ULTRA, to search for a mind control drug that could be weaponized against enemies.

MK-ULTRA, which operated from the 1950s until the early '60s, was created and run by a chemist named Sidney Gottlieb. Journalist Stephen Kinzer, who spent several years investigating the program, calls the operation the "most sustained search in history for techniques of mind control."

Some of Gottlieb's experiments were covertly funded at universities and research centers, Kinzer says, while others were conducted in American prisons and in detention centers in Japan, Germany and the Philippines. Many of his unwitting subjects endured psychological torture ranging from electroshock to high doses of LSD, according to Kinzer's research.

Gottlieb wanted to create a way to seize control of people's minds, and he realized it was a two-part process," Kinzer says. "First, you had to blast away the existing mind. Second, you had to find a way to insert a new mind into that resulting void. We didn't get too far on number two, but he did a lot of work on number one."

Kinzer notes that the top-secret nature of Gottlieb's work makes it impossible to measure the human cost of his experiments. "We don't know how many people died, but a number did, and many lives were permanently destroyed," he says.

Ultimately, Gottlieb concluded that mind control was not possible. After MK-ULTRA shut down, he went on to lead a CIA program that created poisons and high-tech gadgets for spies to use.

Kinzer writes about Gottlieb and MK-ULTRA in his new book, *Poisoner in Chief.*

Interview Highlights

On How the CIA Brought LSD to America
As part of the search for drugs that would allow people to control the human mind, CIA scientists became aware of the existence of LSD, and this became an obsession for the early directors of MK-ULTRA. Actually, the MK-ULTRA director, Sidney Gottlieb, can now be seen as the man who brought LSD to America. He was the unwitting godfather of the entire LSD counterculture.

In the early 1950s, he arranged for the CIA to pay $240,000 to buy the world's entire supply of LSD. He brought this to the United States, and he began spreading it around to hospitals, clinics, prisons and other institutions, asking them, through bogus foundations, to carry out research projects and find out what LSD was, how people reacted to it and how it might be able to be used as a tool for mind control.

Now, the people who volunteered for these experiments and began taking LSD, in many cases, found it very pleasurable. They told their friends about it. Who were those people? Ken Kesey, the author of One Flew Over the Cuckoo's Nest, got his LSD in an experiment sponsored by the CIA by MK-ULTRA, by Sidney Gottlieb. So did Robert Hunter, the lyricist for the Grateful Dead, which went on to become a great purveyor of LSD culture. Allen Ginsberg, the poet who preached the value of the great personal adventure of using LSD, got his first LSD from Sidney Gottlieb. Although, of course, he never knew that name.

So the CIA brought LSD to America unwittingly, and actually it's a tremendous irony that the drug that the CIA hoped would be its key to controlling humanity actually wound up fueling a generational rebellion that was dedicated to destroying everything that the CIA held dear and defended.

On How MK-ULTRA Experimented on Prisoners, Including Crime Boss Whitey Bulger

Whitey Bulger was one of the prisoners who volunteered for what he was told was an experiment aimed at finding a cure for schizophrenia. As part of this experiment, he was given LSD every day for more than a year. He later realized that this had nothing to do with schizophrenia and he was a guinea pig in a government experiment aimed at seeing what people's long-term reactions to LSD was. Essentially, could we make a person lose his mind by feeding him LSD every day over such a long period?

Bulger wrote afterward about his experiences, which he described as quite horrific. He thought he was going insane. He wrote, "I was in prison for committing a crime, but they committed a greater crime on me." And towards the end of his life, Bulger came to realize the truth of what had happened to him, and he actually told his friends that he was going to find that doctor in Atlanta who was the head of that experiment program in the penitentiary and go kill him.

On the CIA Hiring Nazi Doctors and Japanese Torturers to Learn Methods

The CIA mind control project, MK-ULTRA, was essentially a continuation of work that began in Japanese and Nazi concentration camps. Not only was it roughly based on those experiments, but the CIA actually hired the vivisectionists and the torturers who had worked in Japan and in Nazi concentration camps to come and explain what they had found out so that we could build on their research.

For example, Nazi doctors had conducted extensive experiments with mescaline at the Dachau concentration camp, and the CIA was very interested in figuring out whether mescaline could be the key to mind control that was one of their big avenues of investigation. So they hired the Nazi doctors who had been involved in that project to advise them.

Another thing the Nazis provided was information about poison gases like sarin, which is still being used. Nazi doctors came to America to Fort Detrick in Maryland, which was the center of this project, to lecture to CIA officers to tell them how long it took for people to die from sarin.

On the More Extreme Experiments Gottlieb Conducted Overseas

Gottlieb and the CIA established secret detention centers throughout Europe and East Asia, particularly in Japan, Germany and the Philippines, which were largely under American control in the period of the early '50s, and therefore Gottlieb didn't have to worry about any legal entanglements in these places. ...

CIA officers in Europe and Asia were capturing enemy agents and others who they felt might be suspected persons or were otherwise what they called "expendable." They would grab these people and throw them into cells and then test all kinds of, not just drug potions, but other techniques, like electroshock, extremes of temperature, sensory isolation — all the meantime bombarding them with questions, trying to see if they could break down resistance and find a way to destroy the human ego. So these were projects designed not only to understand the human mind but to figure out how to destroy it. And that made Gottlieb, although in some ways a very compassionate person, certainly the most prolific torturer of his generation.

On How These Experiments Were Supervised

[Gottlieb] operated almost completely without supervision. He had sort of a checkoff from his titular boss and from his real boss, Richard Helms, and from the CIA director, Allen Dulles. But none of them really wanted to know what he was doing. This guy had a license to kill. He was allowed to requisition human subjects across the United States and around the world and subject them to any kind of abuse that he wanted, even up to the level of it being fatal — yet nobody looked over his shoulder. He never had to file serious reports to anybody. I think the mentality must have been [that] this project is so important — mind control, if it can be mastered, is the key to global world power.

On How Gottlieb Destroyed Evidence About His Experiments When He Left the CIA

The end of Gottlieb's career came in [1973], when his patron, Richard Helms, who was then director of the CIA, was removed by [President Richard] Nixon. Once Helms was gone, it was just a matter of time until Gottlieb would be gone, and most important was that Helms was really the only person at the CIA who had an idea of what Gottlieb had been doing. So as they were both on their way out of the CIA, they agreed that they should destroy all records of MK-ULTRA. Gottlieb actually drove out to the CIA records center and ordered the archives to destroy boxes full of MK-ULTRA records. ... However, it turns out that there were some [records] found in other places; there was a depot for expense account reports that had not been destroyed, and various other pieces of paper remain. So there is enough out there to reconstruct some of what he did, but his effort to wipe away his traces by destroying all those documents in the early '70s was quite successful.

Periodical and Internet Sources Bibliography

The following articles have been selected to supplement the diverse views presented in this chapter.

"Venona: Soviet Espionage and The American Response 1939-1957," United States Central Intelligence Agency. https://www.cia.gov/static/fc3235f14ff505b6f839321755cfe72d/Venona-Soviet-Espionage-and-The-American-Response-1939-1957.pdf.

Julian E. Barnes and Adam Entous, "How the U.S. Adopted a New Intelligence Playbook to Expose Russia's War Plans," *New York Times,* February 23, 2023. https://www.nytimes.com/2023/02/23/us/politics/intelligence-russia-us-ukraine-china.html.

Amy Davidson Sorkin, "Spooked: What's Wrong with the CIA?" *New Yorker*, October 3, 2022. https://www.newyorker.com/magazine/2022/10/10/has-the-cia-done-more-harm-than-good.

Kat Eschner, "What We Know About the CIA's Midcentury Mind-Control Project," *Smithsonian*, April 13, 2017. https://www.smithsonianmag.com/smart-news/what-we-know-about-cias-midcentury-mind-control-project-180962836.

Michael German, "Strengthening Intelligence Oversight," Brennan Center for Justice, January 27, 2015. https://www.brennancenter.org/our-work/policy-solutions/strengthening-intelligence-oversight.

Danny Haiphong, "CIA Has Given the Human Race Many Reasons to Desire Its Abolition," *Global Times*, October 10, 2022. https://www.globaltimes.cn/page/202210/1276861.shtml.

Olga Khazan, "Gentlemen Reading Each Others' Mail: A Brief History of Diplomatic Spying," the *Atlantic*, June 17, 2013. https://www.theatlantic.com/international/archive/2013/06/gentlemen-reading-each-others-mail-a-brief-history-of-diplomatic-spying/276940/.

Katrina Mulligan and Alexandra Schmitt, "What the Intelligence Community Doesn't Know Is Hurting the United States," Center for American Progress, September 18, 2020. https://www.americanprogress.org/article/intelligence-community-doesnt-know-hurting-united-states.

Jennifer Rubin, "Distinguished Persons of the Week: A Professional Intelligence Community Pays Dividends," *Washington Post,* February 6, 2022. https://www.washingtonpost.com/opinions/2022/02/06/intelligence-community-holding-back-threats-isis-russia/.

David R. Shedd, "The Intelligence Posture America Needs in an Age of Great-Power Competition," Heritage Foundation, November 17, 2020. https://www.heritage.org/military-strength-topical-essays/2021-essays/the-intelligence-posture-america-needs-age-great-power.

Amy Zegart, "Trump vs. the Spies: In Defense of the Intelligence Community," the *Atlantic*, January 6, 2017. https://www.theatlantic.com/international/archive/2017/01/trump-vs-the-spies/512390/.

 Chapter 2

Should Allies Spy on Each Other?

Chapter Preface

When we think of nations engaged in spying, we typically think those nations are spying on their enemies. But it has become apparent in recent years that nations also spy on their friends. The viewpoints in this chapter are primarily concerned with recent revelations that the United States has been spying on its European allies. Specifically, the United States was caught tapping the phones of European leaders, including German chancellor Angela Merkel and French president Emmanuel Macron. The phones of South Korean leaders were also tapped, according to leaked documents.

While spying on friends seems scandalous, authors in this chapter point out that it is not unusual. Security concerns, as you will read in the viewpoint about Denmark's role in U.S. spying on European leaders, often trump loyalty to neighbors and allies. Some authors here argue that spying on allies is necessary and not as bad as it seems. Everyone does it, and everyone knows everyone else does it, some argue. If politics makes strange bedfellows, spying makes even stranger ones. Espionage, as it turns out, is both morally and legally complicated.

Another viewpoint in this chapter takes a close look at the thorny issues involved in diplomacy. The author asks where diplomacy ends and espionage begins. And the answer, according to this author, is not at all straightforward.

The chapter starts out with a viewpoint about allies who work together to do their spying: The Five Eyes alliance of Australia, Canada, New Zealand, the United Kingdom, and the United States. Compared with the controversy over spying *on* allies, spying *with* allies sounds unimpeachable. However, as you will see, the once-secret alliance faces a great deal of criticism.

VIEWPOINT 1

> "The papers documented the mass surveillance programme jointly operated by the Five Eyes to monitor the citizens of member countries."

Five Eyes Nations Surveil Each Other's Citizens

Sumeda Sharma

In this viewpoint, Sumeda Sharma explains what the "Five Eyes" intelligence alliance is in light of a 2023 scandal involving its members. The Five Eyes is a good example of how intelligence gathering in the modern world works among allies. This viewpoint also highlights how quickly this kind of intelligence sharing can get complicated and how the objectives of the Five Eyes has changed over the years. New means of surveillance have raised concerns in the contemporary era over the Five Eyes' methods. Sumeda Sharma is a staff writer for the Hindu, *based in Hyderabad, Telangana, India.*

As you read, consider the following questions:

1. Why was the Five Eyes kept secret for so long?
2. What kinds of intelligence do these nations share?
3. What are some of the criticisms of the alliance that Sharma mentions?

"What is the 'Five Eyes' intelligence alliance? | Explained," by Sumeda Sharma, the *Hindu*, September 27, 2023. Reprinted by permission.

The story so far: The recent allegations by Canadian Prime Minister Justin Trudeau linking the killing of Khalistani leader Hardeep Singh Nijjar on Canadian soil to the Indian government has put the spotlight on the intelligence-sharing alliance 'Five Eyes' (or FVEY), which is believed to have provided the information that "helped" Canada.

In an interview with Canadian CTV News network last week, U.S. Ambassador David Cohen confirmed that there was "shared intelligence among 'Five Eyes' partners that helped lead Canada" to accuse India of "possible" involvement in the killing of the Khalistani separatist. The interview was followed by a report in the *New York Times* on Saturday which said the United States had provided Canada with intelligence but definitive communications intercepted by Ottawa led Mr. Trudeau to accuse India of orchestrating the plot.

"In the aftermath of the killing, U.S. intelligence agencies offered their Canadian counterparts context that helped Canada conclude that India had been involved," the *NYT* reported, quoting sources.

Who Are the 'Five Eyes'?

The 'Five Eyes' is a multilateral intelligence-sharing network shared by over 20 different agencies of five English-speaking countries — Australia, Canada, New Zealand, the United Kingdom and the United States. It is both surveillance-based and signals intelligence (SIGINT). Intelligence documents shared between the member countries are classified 'Secret—AUS/CAN/NZ/UK/US Eyes Only,' which gave the group its title 'Five Eyes.'

How Did the Alliance Come into Being?

The alliance between the U.S. and the U.K. evolved around the Second World War to counter the Cold War Soviet threat. The two countries, which had successfully deciphered German and Japanese codes during the World War, forged a collaboration to share intelligence related to signals such as radio, satellite and internet communications. In the aftermath of the war in 1946, the alliance was formalised through an agreement for cooperation in signals intelligence.

The treaty called the British-U.S. Communication Intelligence Agreement, or BRUSA (now known as the UKUSA Agreement), was signed between the State-Army-Navy Communication Intelligence Board (STANCIB) of the U.S. and the London Signal Intelligence Board (SIGINT) of Britain. Its scope was limited to "communication intelligence matters only" related to "unrestricted" exchange of intelligence products in six areas: collection of traffic; acquisition of communication documents and equipment; traffic analysis; cryptanalysis; decryption and translation; and acquisition of information regarding communication organisations, practices, procedures, and equipment. The arrangement was later extended to 'second party' countries —Canada joined in 1948, while Australia and New Zealand became part of the alliance in 1956.

Though the intelligence alliance came together in the 1940s, it remained a top secret for long. The then Australian PM Gough Whitlam did not know about the existence of BRUSA, regarded as one of the most secret agreements, until 1973, as per a recent article in the *Journal of Cold War Studies*.

In fact, no government officially acknowledged the arrangement by name until 1999 and the text of the agreement was first officially released in public after over 60 years in 2010.

How Does the 'Five Eyes' Network Work?

The five partner countries share a broad range of information and access to their respective intelligence agencies. Initially, the partners are assigned respective SIGINT mandates. A Canadian intelligence officer writes in a military journal (2020) that the US is responsible for Russia, northern China, most of Asia and Latin America; Australia covers southern China, Indo-China and its close neighbours, such as Indonesia; the UK is in charge in Africa and west of the Urals within the former Soviet Union; and New Zealand is responsible for the Western Pacific, while Canada handles the polar regions of Russia.

The goalpost of the Five Eyes, however, has shifted following the collapse of the Soviet Union and the emergence of new global challenges like terrorism and the growing influence of China. For instance, the member countries, except New Zealand, have expressed concern about China's treatment of its Uyghur population in Xinjiang, its threats against Taiwan and suppression of democracy in Hong Kong.

And so, the ambit has widened over to other areas of policy and operations to become a comprehensive, all-source intelligence sharing network. The Five Eyes have become involved in ocean and maritime surveillance, scientific and defence intelligence analysis, medical intelligence, geospatial intelligence, counterintelligence, counterterrorism, and the continuous sharing of intelligence products via a secret collective database known as 'Stone Ghost,' the Canadian officer notes.

To increase cooperation and maintain closeness, the Five Eyes Intelligence Oversight and Review Council (FIORC) was created in September 2016 as the "non-political intelligence oversight, review, and security entities" of the member countries to exchange views on subjects of mutual interest, compare best practices, explore areas of cooperation, and maintain contact with non-Five Eyes countries, among other aims.

What Are the Concerns?

There have been several concerns regarding the privacy, security and methods of working of the intelligence alliance, which remained shrouded in mystery for long. The alliance was embroiled in a major controversy in 2013 following the disclosure of classified documents by Edward Snowden, a former National Security Agency (NSA) contractor.

The papers documented the mass surveillance programme jointly operated by the Five Eyes to monitor the citizens of member countries. Snowden described the network as a "supranational intelligence organisation that doesn't answer to the laws of its own countries."

The U.K.-based charity Privacy International claims that bilateral agreements under the UKUSA reveal the outsourcing of surveillance activities to agencies without limiting their access to classified information. "There is no domestic legislation governing intelligence-sharing, meaning that many of these arrangements lack legal basis and therefore democratic legitimacy. The "third party rule," often included in intelligence-sharing agreements, forbids the disclosure of inter-agency information to third parties, ousting the possibility of oversight," it says.

In 2013, a Canada court rebuked the Canadian Security Intelligence Service (CSIS) for using the alliance to monitor the electronic communications of Canadian terror suspects overseas. The ruling said Canadian spy agencies had deliberately misled judges to expand their eavesdropping powers unlawfully, reported *The Globe and Mail*. Federal agencies were wrongly enlisting U.S. and British allies in global surveillance dragnets that risk harming Canadian terrorism suspects and could expose government agents to criminal charges, the report stated.

Viewpoint 2

> "Espionage is just war and politics played out on a smaller scale by unelected officials and political appointees."

Spying Thrives Under Diplomatic Cover

Eugene Matos and Adrian Zienkiewicz

This viewpoint by Eugene Matos and Adrian Zienkiewicz, first printed in Diplomat Magazine, *takes a look at "diplomatic espionage" and asks where diplomacy ends and spying begins. The viewpoint also explains why, even though spying is illegal, in some cases spies are immune from prosecution. Diplomat Magazine is an international current-affairs magazine for the Asia-Pacific region. It is read by policymakers, academics, and commentators. Eugene Matos works for the International Institute for Middle-East and Balkan Studies and the Geneva Desk for Cooperation and has an extensive legal background. Adrian Zienkiewicz is an international human rights lawyer.*

As you read, consider the following questions:

1. What is the difference between covert operations and covert intelligence, according to this viewpoint?
2. What examples does this viewpoint give of the United States using economic counterintelligence against its allies?

"International Law and Diplomatic Covert Intelligence," by Eugene Matos and Adrian Zienkiewicz, *Diplomat Magazine*, February 21, 2022. Reprinted by permission.

3. What is diplomatic immunity, according to this viewpoint, and why is it problematic?

Most discussion around diplomacy is usually about how they go about representation, however little is discussed about the equally important duty of observing and reporting. It takes big events such as the Raymond Allen Davis case. A contractor with the Central Intelligence Agency (CIA) shot two men killing both in Lahore, Pakistan. In the aftermath, the U.S. government contended that Davis was protected by diplomatic immunity because of his CIA employment with the American consulate in Lahore. The event highlighted a question on the scope of immunities given to consular and diplomatic staff, and more precisely, the role and protections awarded to diplomats working as undercover intelligence agents.

Diplomacy and its legal protection, practices and communication cables, diplomatic bags, have partially, if in theory alone, institutionalized aspects of espionage. Where does diplomacy end and spying begin? Where must one draw the line between official diplomacy and the murky world of espionage? "Every embassy in the world has spies," says University of Buckingham's Prof Anthony Glees during an interview, director of the Centre for Security and Intelligence Studies. Because it is common practice, there's an unwritten understanding that governments are prepared to turn a blind eye to what occurs within embassies. It is a fragile *quid pro quo* between nation-states that has substantial political ramifications.

Most contemporary intelligence officers aren't deeply embedded undercover; these agents are posted as either low or mid-level workers in foreign embassies and monitor affairs from there. The host countries are aware of their actual identities and the types of duties they carry out. They are generally disregarded until they become threats – easier to track the spies you know about than the ones you don't.

In the nuclear, technology and cyberspace era, international law requires constant reinterpretation or reassertion to challenge new problems and adapt to developments in the global system. There are various elements to espionage concerning its purpose, methods, and practices that include these innovative arenas. Excluding armed conflicts, espionage is never explicitly addressed in law; the question is left virtually unanswered. Needless to say, there is a varying consensus by legal scholars regarding its limitations.

What Is Diplomatic Espionage?

With the advent of technology, the practices vary immensely; albeit, it can be defined as a tool for the execution of policy as well as a tool to inform policy, dividing it into two categories: covert operations, which is the tool for the execution of policy, and intelligence, the tool to inform policy. There are two types of espionage in law: covert operations and covert intelligence. Both occur in secrecy to avoid detection, and therefore require significant consideration and preparation.

The first type—covert operations—consists of active and cyberspace operations. States conduct such actions to influence a foreign state. Covert operations remain very classified, which put them in the deep end of espionage. These can be of a coercive nature, and may include, but not be limited to, sabotage, theft, covert political action, and propaganda.

The second type is covert intelligence, the subject of this present analysis and the more obscure strand of diplomatic espionage. It is divided further into two categories: collection of information and analysis of that information. With respect to international law, the initial collection of information raises considerable legal questions, making it highly contested, especially for diplomats whose primary function is to listen and report. Accordingly, both mandates, covert intelligence and diplomacy, are interested in gathering vital and classified foreign information through different techniques, of private and public nature, for strategic policy goals. Usually, the distinction is perceived through the methods used and the targets in mind, is where the line of malpractice in diplomacy is drawn.

Why Is It Important?
Foreign data collection itself has several variants and they are used to guide foreign policy and apprehend the future behaviour of its constituents not only in military applications, but also in trade and investments, as well as general regional politics. Thus, intelligence gathering is a crucial practice towards the greater ambitions of a state, and its secrecy further implies that intelligence is integral in the state decision-making process.

A Question of Diplomatic Practice
The issue is rightfully not whether diplomats can spy or not; rather, one should understand the limitations. Espionage, economic and industrial intelligence remains a missing dimension of international affairs, diplomatic history and its study. Diplomatic espionage is also practiced between friendly states, 'friendly' economic espionage is seen as a covert activity between competing foreign states to acquire economic intelligence used to interfere with certain states' economic opportunities. These are popular variables in trade negotiations. The USA has successfully used macroeconomic, microeconomic and economic counterintelligence against its allies. In fact the *New York Times* confirmed that the United States has expanded the role of American diplomats in collecting intelligence overseas. Case in point, United States diplomats were directly instructed to spy on United Nations, and EU leaders, as confirmed by Wikileaks, a 2009 confidential directive from the United States Department of State.

Is Diplomatic Covert Intelligence Legal?
Diplomatic immunity is a form of legal immunity that ensures diplomats are given safe passage in the host country. Diplomats are unsusceptible to lawsuits or prosecution under the host country's laws. Although the practice of espionage is technically illegal, it is forgivable by law for diplomats, yet the line between ethical practice does affect contemporary diplomatic relations when crossed arbitrarily. In certain cases, states knowingly cross this

line despite high geopolitical stakes, with considerable aftermath as seen with the Snowden leak in Venezuela/Germany/USA relations.

A diplomat has the conventional duty, by nature and mandate, to observe the receiving state. However, some diplomats have lurked away from the light and gone into endeavours that are incompatible with their official plan, such as infiltration, development of cover identities, or by monitoring the behaviours of individuals or groups to gather information and persuade political disenchantment. In correlation, we accord an interest to the instructive case of legal resident spies operating in a foreign state with an official cover and protection of a member of a diplomatic mission, which is yes protected by law. However, the law creates a clear distinction if the member is a consular or diplomat.

Consular Staff?

Immunity is a product of the Vienna Convention on Consular/Diplomatic Relations, 1963/61, and the International Law Commission. To begin with consular agents, they are accountable to all state laws except for a few functional circumstances. In addition, a consular officer's protection is limited to reporting and performing intelligence functions by all lawful means and can only report on the conditions and developments of the receiving State's commercial, economic, cultural and scientific life.

Moreover, the Vienna Convention on Consular Relations, 1963 (VCCR) art 43 ss. 1 states that consular staff are "not amenable to the jurisdiction of the judicial or administrative authorities of the receiving State in respect of acts performed in the exercise of consular functions" and that they should only be liable to arrest, according to article 41, "in the case of a grave crime and pursuant to a decision by the competent judicial authority".

In other words, the law has given us parameters for consular agents to respect these: intelligence from resident accredited consular staff is legal under the VCCR 1963 insofar that, the consular mission respects the laws of the receiving State, that the activities do not include illegal covert operations, that the activities are restricted to observe and report (intelligence) in matters within the function of the consulate and that the intelligence is restricted to only the socio-economic development of the host state.

Diplomatic Staff

If a diplomatic member assigned to an embassy is caught crossing the line in espionage, the host authorities would have to admit the principle of diplomatic immunity, by which diplomatic officials are not subject to the jurisdiction of local courts and other authorities for both their official and, to a large extent, their personal activities. The Vienna Convention on Diplomatic Relations 1961, offers broader protections than the consulate. For example, the archives and documents of a diplomatic mission are inviolable and shall not be seized or opened by the host government (Article 24).

The host country must permit and protect free communication between the diplomats of the mission and their home country. A diplomatic bag must never be opened, even on suspicion of abuse, and a diplomatic courier must never be arrested or detained (Article 27). Diplomats must not be liable to any form of arrest or detention, and the receiving state must make all efforts to protect their person and dignity (Article 29). Diplomats are immune from the civil and criminal jurisdiction of the host state, with exceptions for professional activities outside the diplomat's official functions (Article 31). Therefore, the only clear path to prosecution offered is Article 32, permitting sending states to waive this immunity.

It is safe to assume that the repercussions vary enormously giving us a plethora of options if a diplomat gets caught crossing the line. Detention, interrogation and the possibility of a trial in a public venue are not usually possible for diplomats. Again, the factors depend on the government in question, who the diplomat is working for, their citizenship, and what information they may have received or transferred. Thus we switch to the political context.

If a diplomat gets caught crossing the line of what's acceptable, but they're not causing noteworthy harm, usually they'll just get kicked out of the country and sent back home; these actions are swift. Getting caught red handed is the genesis of a wave of political humiliation and negative diplomatic relations. In the case of diplomatic immunity, an intelligence operator would be, in general, only answerable to the jurisdiction of the host state if the sending state waives off the diplomatic immunity.

Repercussions for Non-Diplomats?

However, once a spy crosses the line and they do not carry or diplomatic immunity is waived, it's game on. If it's an ally that has compromised defenses, an exchange or kicked out of the country, and if it's a citizen to the host country a lengthy jail term is likely in store. The ally, too embarrassed about getting caught, no one wants to cause an international diplomatic incident over something they were trying to keep hush-hush in the first place. Enemy spies are slightly different, and their fates largely depend on the relationship between the two nations. They also make good bargaining chips – even bitter enemies have been known to trade captured spies. Whenever an enemy spy gets sent back to his home country, it's usually because someone wanted to keep the peace.

Espionage is just war and politics played out on a smaller scale by unelected officials and political appointees. Accordingly, the fate of any one agent is largely determined by negotiations, the political environment and of course diplomacy. Spying is illegal as per the national law of almost every state, but some foreigners can be protected or immune to those laws, insofar that the method of covert intelligence fits in the parameters of the principles of diplomatic or functions of the consular immunity.

VIEWPOINT 3

> "Another useful spillover of the spying 'scandal' is that it has initiated a much-needed wider discussion about balancing concerns over individual privacy with counter-terrorism."

Spying Among Friends Raises Concerns
Daniel Baldino

This viewpoint by Daniel Baldino discusses two situations that took place in 2013 in which countries were caught spying on their allies: the United States spying on Germany, and Australia spying on Indonesia. Both situations caused a scandal, and Baldino discusses the contrasting responses from the leaders of both countries. Barack Obama—who was the U.S. president at that time—recognized that the incident reflected poorly on the United States and acknowledged it as a faux pas, promising to take action to reevaluate the country's intelligence practices, while Tony Abbott—who was prime minister of Australia at that time—defended his country's actions in the name of national security. Baldino asserts that spying on allies is diplomatic ground that needs to be tread carefully, despite the fact that many countries engage in it. Daniel Baldino is a senior lecturer in politics and international relations at the University of Notre Dame, Australia.

"Spying Scandal: Obama, Abbott, and Why Sorry Is the Hardest Word to Say," by Daniel Baldino, The Conversation November 20, 2013, https://theconversation.com/spying-scandal-obama-abbott-and-why-sorry-is-the-hardest-word-to-say-20555. Licensed under CC BY-ND 4.0 International.

Espionage and Intelligence

As you read, consider the following questions:

1. Does Baldino believe President Obama was being honest when he said he was unaware that U.S. intelligence was spying on then-German chancellor Angela Merkel? Why or why not?
2. What does Baldino say is wrong with the nationalistic rhetoric that has surrounded discussions of national security and intelligence since the 9/11 attacks?
3. What does Baldino argue is the best way for a leader to react when their country is caught spying on an ally?

The contrast between Australian prime minister Tony Abbott's self-defeating response to spying allegations with Indonesia and US president Barack Obama's reaction to smooth its similar row with Germany is eye-catching.

Obama wasted little time in getting on the front foot and attempted to mitigate the mix of offence and indignation from European leaders and the public. While much of this outrage should be seen as both hypocritical and part of standard political theatre – and despite the fact that signals intelligence might be a useful part of regular US operations – the White House was sensitive to containing wider anti-US sentiment and backlash.

In contrast, Abbott needs to better filter his natural bulldog political instincts, and should apologise to Indonesia. The clear-eyed combative stance that served him well as opposition leader can do more harm than good when dealing with the intricacies and complexities of foreign affairs.

This is not to suggest being assertive and even being prepared to occasionally get noses out of joint is an unimportant tool in the rough-and-tumble world of diplomacy.

The Obama Example

Obama acted to take the protests against US spying activities seriously. He did not throw up "national security" smokescreens. He issued a personal apology to German chancellor Angela Merkel and ordered an immediate and total "review" of the activities of the intelligence community. He suggested a preparedness to find ways to do things differently with like-minded partners than from the past.

It is also likely that Obama was being half honest when he stated an unawareness of the specifics of the particular operations that had intercepted Merkel's phone calls. The US president's job is not to micromanage the intelligence community (including the selection of targets), although he certainly would have been fundamentally aware that the US is spying on foreign leaders abroad.

Yet despite the expressions of US willingness for self-imposed limits to its foreign policy activities, it is unlikely that we will witness a radical overall change in the ways and means of US espionage based on the latest diplomatic row. But hopefully the breach of trust might allow for some wider self-reflection about the costs, not just the benefits, of the rise of the surveillance state.

Another useful spillover of the spying "scandal" is that it has initiated a much-needed wider discussion about balancing concerns over individual privacy with counter-terrorism. It has also sparked a debate on whether agencies are collecting data because it is critical to inform relevant decisions or simply because they can do.

But the immediate point in this particular instance of Obama's diplomatic outreach was to distinguish quickly between friend from foe, and promise to set or review some national rules to calm people's suspicion and fear about US power.

It is worth acknowledging that Obama's pitch to placate overseas audiences rather than justify the case for unlimited

> ## Revelations of Spying Won't Affect Relations with Allies, U.S. Says
>
> The US is arguing that the recent leak of classified intelligence documents does not contain anything that damages the alliance with South Korea.
> "We have engaged with our allies and partners since these leaks came out, and we have done so at high levels, and we have made clear our commitment to safeguarding intelligence and our commitment to our security partnerships," US Secretary of State Tony Blinken said at a press conference in Vietnam on Saturday.
> "What I've heard so far at least is an appreciation for the steps that we're taking, and it's not affected our cooperation," Blinken continued, emphasizing that he had "not heard anything that would affect our cooperation with allies and partners."
> Although the leak of the classified US intelligence documents raised suspicions of Washington having eavesdropped on discussions held by officials in South Korea's National Security Office, the government in Seoul has yet to express any regret about the incident.
> Regarding these suspicions, the National Security Office's first deputy director, Kim Tae-hyo, told reporters on Tuesday at Dulles International Airport near Washington that the office "hasn't found any evidence of ill will from our ally the US."
> The South Korean government is also drawing the line at the possibility of putting the eavesdropping allegations on the agenda at the upcoming South Korea-US summit.

surveillance was not without some domestic heartburn. There has been various murmurings from intelligence agencies that Obama failed to adequately defend spies for doing their job and responding to executive priorities.

There has been no support for the agency (NSA) from the President or his staff or senior administration officials, and this has not gone unnoticed by both senior officials and the rank and file at the Fort.

However, according to a report by the Associated Press, the intelligence leak is casting a shadow on Blinken's upcoming attendance at the G7 foreign ministers meeting to be held in Karuizawa, Nagano, Japan this Sunday through Wednesday.

While previously serving as secretary of state, Hillary Clinton also had to explain the US government's position to countries like Argentina, Israel, and Italy in the wake of the WikiLeaks incident in 2010, which involved a significant leak of US intelligence documents and also revealed controversial US wiretapping activities abroad.

Meanwhile, an article published by the Wall Street Journal on Saturday explained how the US has been facing major difficulties in renewing Section 702 of the Foreign Intelligence Surveillance Act. This particular section allows US intelligence agencies to conduct intelligence activities, including but not limited to wiretapping, abroad.

In other words, US intelligence agencies are authorized to carry out intelligence activities in other countries, under Section 702, which, in turn, is supervised by a special foreign intelligence surveillance court that approves the rules the program operates under.

The section, however, is set to expire later this year unless the US Congress reauthorizes it.

According to experts quoted by the *Wall Street Journal,* Congress is, at the minimum, hinting at the possibility of strengthening the control system in response to this incident.

"Blinken says indications of US spying won't affect cooperation with allies," by Jung E-gil, *The Hankyoreh*, April 17, 2023.

What Abbott Can Learn

Based on glimpses of Abbott's approach to diplomacy, he appears a closer disciple of the George W. Bush school of modern diplomacy: a "my-way-or-the-highway" point of view.

While it is true that all countries spy on each other, it is Australia that has been caught out in this instance. At the very least, swift signals that displayed a willingness to listen to the concerns of others are all part of the ebb and flow of a larger political game – especially when the "victim" (in this case, Indonesia) is a crucial ally.

More broadly, contrite public explanations can help to avoid inflaming an Asian audience. Australia has traditionally had a long-standing image problem in some parts of Asia, such as the US "deputy sheriff" tag that appears very hard to remove.

Smart diplomacy also requires nuanced cues and forward-thinking, especially when dealing with fragile but vitally important relationships like Australia and Indonesia. Compromise or a preparedness to make assurances about future policy directions – or even eating some humble pie – should not be automatically equated with weakness and the undermining of national interests.

A "call-to-arms" nationalistic rhetoric – that has worked generally well for politicians in domestic settings in the post 9/11 world – lacks diplomatic finesse and, in this instance, reeks of hubris.

An apology to Indonesia should be the first step as part of the Australian government's priority to reduce the impact of the spying revelations on Indonesian national pride and not back their policymakers into a corner where they feel compelled – in part due to democratic considerations – to respond in an equally pointed and sharp public manner. It's a lose-lose situation.

The well-established script that the Australian government does not comment on (or show contrition for) intelligence matters is getting tiresome. In this instance, it is hardly a justification for diplomatic negligence and failing to exercise political self-restraint.

VIEWPOINT 4

> "This scandal might provide an opportunity for Denmark to take an honest look at its security and defence priorities—and its relations with European allies."

The Need for Security Can Cause Allies to Make Controversial Choices

Amelie Theussen

The plot thickens, regarding the United States spying on allies. In this viewpoint, Amelie Theussen describes how Denmark aided the U.S. when it spied on its European allies, including France, Germany, Norway, and Sweden. Theussen argues that Denmark needs the support of the U.S. because the EU does not yet have the resources to defend the country against Russia and China. (Note that this viewpoint was written in 2021, before Russia invaded Ukraine.) While maintaining good relations with the U.S. is important to the country's security, maintaining positive relationships with its European allies and neighbors is as well, and Theussen asserts that this scandal offers Denmark the opportunity to reassess its diplomatic priorities. Amelie Theussen is an assistant professor at the Center for War Studies, University of Southern Denmark.

"Why did Denmark help the US spy on its European allies?," by Amelie Theussen, The Conversation, June 8, 2021. https://theconversation.com/why-did-denmark-help-the-us-spy-on-its-european-allies-161959. Licensed under CC BY-ND 4.0 International.

As you read, consider the following questions:

1. How did Denmark assist the NSA in spying on European heads of state?
2. Why was Denmark a particularly good partner for the U.S. in this operation?
3. Why, according to this viewpoint, might Denmark have been willing to take this risk?

"Systematic wiretapping of close allies is unacceptable," came a recent comment from Danish Defence Minister Trine Bramsen. And yet, it appears this is exactly what Denmark has been doing. Bramsen was responding to reporting that revealed the Danish Defence Intelligence Service (Forsvarets Efterretningstjeneste, or FE) had cooperated with the US National Security Agency (NSA) to enable spying on several European partners and close allies.

Considering the major reputational costs that would surely have been evident from the outset, why did Denmark agree to this partnership? Why would it allow the NSA to use Danish data cables to spy on senior officials in France, Germany, Norway and Sweden, including German chancellor Angela Merkel?

For a Danish audience this scandal is part of a longer story. In 2019, the independent board overseeing Danish intelligence services (Tilsynet med Efterretningtjenesterne, created in 2014 after the Edward Snowden leaks) received information about the FE collaborating with the NSA. The board produced a report in August 2020 criticising the intelligence service for serious wrongdoings.

Still little is known of the board's strictly confidential four-volume report, which was submitted to Bramsen, but its press statement publicly criticised the FE for initiating "operational activities in violation of Danish law, including by obtaining and passing on a significant amount of information about Danish citizens."

As a result of the report, five top intelligence officials were removed from office. A few months later, media reports revealed that the collaboration had enabled the NSA not only to spy on neighbouring countries' officials, but also Danish ministries and defence companies.

The exact nature of the retrieved information and how it was used is unclear but the fact that any information of this kind was gathered at all is in complete contrast to the FE's purpose to prevent and counter threats to Denmark and Danish interests.

The most recent media reporting suggests in more detail that the FE had collaborated with the NSA to allow the US to spy on neighbouring countries though Danish internet cables between 2012 and 2014. It was revealed that the NSA was purposefully targeting high-ranking European officials, using their phone numbers as "selectors" to identify data of interest.

Why Chance It?

Denmark's geographical location makes the country attractive for the NSA, not least because it hosts several key underwater cables for neighbouring countries. These cables can be used to get information about not only internet access, chats and messaging services, but also text messages and phone calls.

When considering why Denmark would allow itself to become a conduit for espionage against its allies, it's worth remembering that, as a small country, it is dependent on security guarantees from other states. Denmark has aligned itself closely with the US – the world's largest military superpower – not just through NATO, but also bilaterally. For Denmark, the cooperation with the US and the NSA is crucial, both in terms of technology and access to intelligence.

The FE is highly dependent on the NSA to combat terrorism. Through the NSA, it gains access to advanced technology such as the program Xkeyscore, used to search through and filter the raw data from the cables. It also seems that the FE had access to information about planned terror attacks via the NSA.

Even though progress has been made on the European side in regard to increasing cooperation on security and defence matters,

Nato and particularly the US continue to be Denmark's most important security guarantor.

Since the 1990s, but particularly since 9/11, Danish foreign policy has been described as "super-atlanticist" – prioritising building common values and interests with the US. This "strong and seemingly unwavering support for the American world order" means Denmark is "willing to pursue costly and risky policies to support the superpower."

Additionally, Denmark remains to a large extent outside European Union security and defence cooperation because of its defence opt-out. Negotiated after the Danish population rejected the Maastricht Treaty in a referendum in 1992, the defence opt-out prevents the country from participating in those parts of the EU's foreign and security policy that affect defence and any military cooperation at EU level.

This puts the relationship to the US (and Nato) at the forefront of Danish security and defence decision-making. Nor does the EU (yet) have the strength to defend itself against Russia and China should the need arise, which in part explains the draw of the US partnership.

Facing the Music

The French government described the allegations against Denmark as "extremely serious", with President Emmanuel Macron pointing out that "this is not acceptable between allies, and even less between allies and European partners."

Merkel agrees, but has struck a more conciliatory tone, seeing "a good basis not only for the resolution of the matter, but also to really come to trusted relations". However, Peer Steinbrück, former German opposition leader and candidate for chancellor, called it a political scandal.

Even closer to home, Norwegian Prime Minister Erna Solberg said "it is unacceptable if countries which have close allied cooperation feel the need to spy on one another". Peter Hultqvist, Sweden's defence minister, has demanded "full information".

Much of these events date back to the time of the Snowden years, when it was revealed that even Germany's foreign intelligence agency cooperated with the NSA to spy on its neighbours. It thus remains to be seen how much damage will really be done to Denmark's relations with the rest of Europe. A government-commissioned investigation is due to report back later in 2021.

However, it may be that this scandal might provide an opportunity for Denmark to take an honest look at its security and defence priorities – and its relations with European allies. A recent poll shows that 66% of Danes believe that Europe cannot always rely on the US and needs to look after its own defence capabilities. This puts Denmark's super-atlanticist orientation into question and suggests its most important strategic partners may lie closer to home.

VIEWPOINT 5

> "We must be realistic: our allies have acted, act, and will continue to act secretly or opaquely in ways that materially affect our interests. So we have good reasons to know what they are up to and spying may be the best or only way to get at that information."

There Are Times When We Must Spy on Our Allies

Elbridge Colby

When the U.S. was caught spying on its allies, European leaders denounced the practice. However, it's not clear how much of the outrage was genuine. In this viewpoint, Elbridge Colby argues that spying on allies is necessary, and no one should be offended by it. Even though these countries are considered allies to the U.S., they also present their own threats to U.S. national security and diplomatic interests, and it is unlikely these countries will be forthcoming about these issues. Elbridge Colby is an American national security policy expert and former Deputy Assistant Secretary of Defense.

"Why We Must Spy on Our Allies," by Elbridge Colby, *The National Interest*, December 4, 2013. Reprinted by permission.

Should Allies Spy on Each Other?

As you read, consider the following questions:

1. Colby says the U.S. shouldn't be offended that its allies aren't perfectly honest with them. Why not?
2. According to this viewpoint, what may have motivated the U.S. to spy on Germany?
3. What are some of the threats from the U.S.'s allies, according to Colby, that warrant keeping a close eye on them?

The recent uproar over the NSA's alleged tapping of German chancellor Angela Merkel's cell phone has brought to a crescendo cries that U.S. intelligence collection activities have gone too far—and not just at home, but abroad. Influential members of Congress and leading opinion makers are going so far as to call for a prohibition on spying on U.S. allies. Indeed, news reports suggest that the president may ban at least some forms of such surveillance (and may have already taken steps in that direction), and that the American people might well support such a step.

This would be a big mistake. No doubt there is or has been some imprudent and perhaps even inappropriate spying on allies. And it is up to us to keep such activities secret or, at the very least, out of the headlines. But as a rule, the United States *should* be prepared to collect intelligence on its allies.

Why? The U.S. government should collect foreign intelligence to fulfill its most important role, which is to protect the security, liberty and well-being of its citizens. Collecting intelligence on our allies is sometimes necessary to fulfill this obligation, because what allies do and what happens within their borders can and regularly does have a major impact on Americans. Let's remember what being a U.S. ally actually means: that American citizens are committed to defending these countries with their resources and ultimately with their lives. So, since our allies see fit to ask us to defend them, we have a reasonable interest in knowing what they are up to.

Now, if our allies were perfectly transparent and straightforward with us, there would be no problem. But they aren't. Nor should we be particularly surprised or offended by this. After all, *our own* government doesn't meet this standard. Bear in mind that Congress regularly complains that the executive branch is hiding information from it and that, even within the executive, information sharing is a huge challenge.

More to the point, *nobody expects* allies to be fully transparent or entirely open with each other. After all, alliances are mutual-defense pacts grounded in conceptions of self-interest broadly understood, not political unions or pledges of Kantian fidelity. Allies remain separate governments and pursue their own interests. And they pursue those interests in ways at best opaque to their allies and, quite often, by actively trying to hide their activities even from friendly governments.

This means that there are situations in which the U.S. government has a legitimate need to know what our allies are up to or what is going on within their borders but in which our allies don't or can't know what is going on or won't be transparent with us. It is in these situations that it is not only appropriate for but incumbent upon the U.S. government to collect information on or about our allies.

What do these situations look like? In their most innocent form, things may happen within the territory or even the governments of allies that we may care about but which our ally is ignorant of or unable or unwilling to track down. For instance, allies may be ignorant of a threat to us (and possibly them)—recall that the 9/11 attacks were partially plotted out in Hamburg. Or allies may be incapable of collecting intelligence on agreed, known threats—such as the Philippines' difficulties in dealing with the terrorist Abu Sayyaf Group. Or we may see a threat where our allies don't, blocking cooperative action and intelligence sharing—witness U.S.-European differences in attitudes towards the threats posed by Hezbollah and Hamas. Or our allies may lack the resolve we see as crucial to dealing with a threat—see "major non-NATO ally" Pakistan's underwhelming initiatives against radical jihadists.

Nor are such concerns limited to terrorism. Foreign governments might be unwittingly penetrated by hostile intelligence services, as Germany was during the Cold War, or serve as unknowing transit routes for proliferation or other noxious activities, or be hobbled by radical or anti-American factions.

But such situations may arise for less innocent reasons as well. Being allied doesn't entail always harmonizing policies, and it doesn't mean always telling the whole truth. In fact, our allies can and often do disagree with us and they often pursue policies we don't like—and they sometimes do so on matters that implicate our dollars, our reputation, and, most importantly, our lives. And they may pursue these policies opaquely or in secret.

Just take Germany, the focus of the current controversy. Germany is one of the most important and steadfast U.S. allies, and we should make every effort to keep it as one. Yet since World War II, Germany has seriously considered pursuing its own nuclear weapons capability, flirted with unilateral rapprochement with the Soviet Union, stirred European fears during reunification in the 1990s, and stridently opposed U.S. action against Iraq in the 2000s. All of these issues, and many more like them, were questions in which the United States had highly important interests at stake and thus very good reasons to want to know how Germany might behave.

And of course Germany is not a special case. Other allies have surprised Washington by going to war or coming close to it, pursued covert nuclear-weapons programs, and surreptitiously tried to undermine U.S. peace efforts. Moreover, alliances are not undying. Observe the dramatic shifts away from the United States that de Gaulle initiated in France in the 1960s or that the Ayatollah Khomeini brought about after the overthrow of the Shah. And it is worth noting that the U.S. government was surprised by the Iranian

Revolution precisely because it had so sharply limited intelligence collection within the country under the Shah, then considered a close and reliable ally. Given that we have been haranguing the Intelligence Community since 9/11 for failures of imagination and the inability to "anticipate surprise," wouldn't it be unwise to hamstring their reasonable ability to do so?

Nor are these concerns merely historical. There are plenty of instances today in which American interests could be affected, potentially seriously so, by the decisions of allies with whom our relations are not characterized by translucent openness. To name just a few: Japan and the Philippines are engaged in fervent territorial disputes with megapower China; South Korea has pledged it will respond forcefully to North Korean attacks; Middle East partners appear prepared to do the same in the face of Iranian provocations; and the Baltic states have long-running disputes with Putin's Russia. We rightly take the side of our allies in each of these disputes, but a realistic look reveals that our interests and policies and those of our allies do not always fully coincide, and sometimes diverge considerably. Given that any of those scenarios could lead to a crisis or even conflict, ones in which the United States would be expected to come to its allies' aid (and remember that some of those potential adversaries can not only attack American forces abroad but can strike with devastating force at the American homeland), don't we have excellent reasons to gain as clear an understanding as possible of how our allies are going to act?

This is not to say that the United States should conduct unrestricted or even necessarily very active spying on its allies. And there are certainly allies which we might well reasonably conclude are not worth spying on, such as the vaunted "Five Eyes" group. And it is *certainly* not to say that we should conduct spying designed to hurt or undermine our allies—that would defeat the point of our alliances and would be against the better angels of our nature. We want our allies to do well and to maintain strong and positive relations with them. For these reasons, we should work through regular channels where and when possible to understand what our allies are up to and what is going on within their borders. This is both sensible, given the dangers of getting caught and the attendant political blowback we see exemplified in the Merkel imbroglio, but is also in accord with our political traditions of promoting open and rule-bound government.

But at the same time, we must be realistic: our allies have acted, act, and will continue to act secretly or opaquely in ways that materially affect our interests. So we have good reasons to know what they are up to and spying may be the best or only way to get at that information.

This need has the firmest domestic legal justification in the Constitution's mandate to the government to protect Americans. And it's worth remembering that our Founding Fathers thought spying on and manipulating our allies was not just appropriate but necessary; there is a reason why the CIA sees Ben Franklin, whose machinations in Paris were instrumental to our successful Revolution, as the Founding Father of covert action. But our justifications are not confined merely to our own self-interest or traditions. Rather, an obvious additional justification is that our allies spy on us, and often do so far more enthusiastically than we do.

But a more principled reason than "you do it too" is that American intelligence collection is a crucial part of America's broader security posture, and that security posture has underwritten not only our own *but also our allies'* security for almost seven decades now. We don't just collect intelligence so that we can secure ourselves; we collect intelligence so that we can secure the many countries we're committed to defending. And doing that effectively means more than just collecting intelligence on our potential enemies. Bear in mind that many of our allies have feared not only the Soviet Union or Iran or North Korea—but have also feared *each other*. Thus a crucial part of U.S. security policy since 1945 has been managing and reducing tensions among our allies, including allies with bitter memories and clashing interests. Once again, take the case of Germany and remember that NATO's first

Secretary General summarized common European thinking in describing NATO's basic purpose: to "keep the Americans in, the Russians out, and the Germans down."

Nor is this merely an historical problem—observe the deep tensions today between U.S. allies South Korea and Japan or between Israel and the Gulf nations. And just as overweening American military power has over time reassured many of our allies that they could rely on the United States to insure them against the possibility of resurgent German, Japanese or Turkish military power, so too do formidable U.S. intelligence collection capabilities contribute to that reassurance. Nor do the Germanys and Japans of our alliance structure suffer from this. Quite the contrary, they have no better way of persuading their neighbors of their good faith than American oversight.

It is crucial to maintain our ability to spy on allies, but misguided excessive pressure from our allies might well persuade us to make a bad decision to constrain or even suspend this ability. We should therefore not be shy about making these points, both here and in the international arena. Of course, these arguments presume some degree of trustworthiness and even benevolence on the part of the United States. But is such presumption unreasonable? Has the United States used its military and intelligence power for or against the interests of its allies? Have they benefited or suffered from it? Certainly we should not be given carte blanche—as Americans, we are believers in checks and balances. But these points do suggest that our allies should think very carefully before pressing the United States too far on this matter.

Ultimately, though, Americans should decide for themselves whether their government should be prepared to spy on allies. One option would be to return to the policy of "gentlemen don't read each other's mail" that we (at least partially) adhered to in the 1930s, a decade not distinguished by the wisdom of its foreign policies. But while a public prohibition on spying on our allies would certainly represent a noisy gesture of our idealism, it would not represent a judicious one. The other option would be to retain our ability to collect intelligence on or about our allies, but to redouble our intention to do so only for sound and defensible reasons. The latter course, while perhaps a somewhat deflating admission of the enduring imperfection of life in the international arena, represents the prudent course.

Periodical and Internet Sources Bibliography

The following articles have been selected to supplement the diverse views presented in this chapter.

Natasha Bertrand and Kylie Atwood, "Leaked Pentagon Documents Provide Rare Window into Depth of US Intelligence on Allies and Foes," CNN Politics, April 10, 2023. https://www.cnn.com/2023/04/09/politics/pentagon-leaked-documents-us-spying-allies-foes/index.html.

Elisabeth Braw, "Spying on Allies Is Normal. Also Smart." *Politico*, June 4, 2021. https://www.politico.eu/article/spying-allies-normal-us-denmark/.

Krishnadev Calamur, "4 Things to Know About Spying on Allies," NPR, October 28, 2013. https://www.npr.org/sections/parallels/2013/10/28/241384089/four-things-to-know-about-spying-on-allies.

Chantal Da Silva, "Merkel, Macron Demand Answers on Report Denmark Helped U.S. Spy on Allies," NBC News, June 1, 2021. https://www.nbcnews.com/news/world/merkel-macron-demand-answers-report-denmark-helped-u-s-spy-n1269214.

Steve Inskeep, "The U.S. Intelligence Leaks Have Sparked Outrage in South Korea," NPR, April 13, 2023. https://www.npr.org/2023/04/13/1169648741/the-u-s-intelligence-leaks-have-sparked-outrage-in-south-korea.

Jeong-Ho Lee, "Seoul Dismisses Report of US Spying on Allies, Says Ties Strong," *Bloomberg*, April 9, 2023. https://www.bloomberg.com/news/articles/2023-04-09/seoul-dismisses-report-of-us-spying-on-allies-says-ties-strong.

Hanako Montgomery, "Leaked Docs Show U.S. Spying on Its Allies, and No One Should Be Surprised," *Vice News*, April 12, 2023, https://www.vice.com/en/article/5d9bp8/us-spies-allies-south-korea-pentagon-leak.

Missy Ryan, Ellen Nakashima, and John Hudson, "Allies Troubled by Document Leak, but Need U.S. Spying Capabilities," *Washington Post,* April 14, 2023. https://www.washingtonpost.com/national-security/2023/04/14/us-intelligence-leak-allies/.

Margaret Warner, "An Exclusive Club: The 5 Countries that Don't Spy on Each Other," PBS, October 25, 2013. https://www.pbs.org/newshour/world/an-exclusive-club-the-five-countries-that-dont-spy-on-each-other.

Calvin Yang, "Recent Intel Leak Shows US Spies on Not Only Their Foes, but Their Allies too: Analysts," Channel News Asia, April 10, 2023. https://www.channelnewsasia.com/world/confidential-intelligence-document-leak-united-states-spies-adversaries-allies-3408081.

CHAPTER 3

Should the Government Spy on Its Own Citizens?

Chapter Preface

The previous chapter examined the issues of governments spying on their allies. Revelations that the United States had tapped the phones of leaders of its allies created a minor diplomatic crisis. However, that is small potatoes compared to what the authors in this chapter discuss. Here, the focus is on governments spying on their own citizens.

After the 9/11 attacks of 2001, the U.S. government began programs and policies intended to deter terrorist attacks. Though doing so was crucial, in trying to nab foreign terrorists, government officials used methods that violated the rights of American citizens. Still, Americans were shocked when Edward Snowden revealed the massive program of spying on U.S. citizens being conducted by the U.S. National Security Agency (NSA). Since then, according to a viewpoint here, changes have been made to the program, but they seem more like gestures than actual reforms. Not much, it seems, has changed.

Some of the authors in this chapter take a close look at that particular surveillance program and the difficulty the U.S. Congress is having in deciding how much surveillance of American citizens to allow. Others zero in specifically on Edward Snowden, the intelligence analyst who leaked classified information about the NSA's surveillance program. Was Snowden a whistleblower or a traitor?

In one way or another, all the viewpoints in this chapter address the question of how much freedom and privacy Americans need to give up in order to stay safe, and more important, who gets to make that decision?

VIEWPOINT 1

> "When the government collects foreigners' information, it inevitably scoops up Americans' communications, too. The government deems this 'incidental' collection, but agents can still access and search this data without a warrant."

The NSA Has Made Changes to Spying Programs — but Not Enough

Sarah Childress

In this viewpoint, journalist Sarah Childress looks at changes made in the NSA spying program since Edward Snowden leaked information showing the extent to which the U.S. had been spying on its own citizens. Since the scandal erupted, the government has implemented some changes in the program. Childress investigates how helpful those changes have been and whether they are simply gestures to appease concerned American citizens and politicians. Childress argues that although changes have been made, they do not go far enough to protect the privacy of U.S. citizens. Sarah Childress is currently deputy editor for long-term investigations at the Washington Post.

"How the NSA Spying Programs Have Changed Since Snowden," by Sarah Childress, Frontline, February 9, 2015. Reprinted by permission.

Should the Government Spy on Its Own Citizens?

As you read, consider the following questions:

1. How is the privacy of Americans being violated if the NSA is targeting non-U.S. citizens?
2. What did the U.S. government mean by "appropriate safeguards"? Do the sources cited here think these safeguards are enough?
3. How is the FBI involved in intelligence-gathering by the NSA?

In the wake of Edward Snowden's June 2013 leaks, President Barack Obama promised to review the government's surveillance programs and consider reforms.

"It's not enough for me, as president, to have confidence in these programs," he said in August of that year. "The American people need to have confidence in them as well."

Obama tasked five policy and security experts with reviewing the government's surveillance capabilities. He also asked his Privacy and Civil Liberties Oversight Board, another five-member team, to review and make recommendations on two controversial programs Snowden exposed — the bulk telephone record collection, known as Section 215, and the program that allows spying on non-U.S. citizens, Section 702.

The two groups have issued a number of reports, and the administration has also released its own assessments, including a January 2014 presidential policy directive announcing some policy changes.

Last week, the Office of the Director of National Intelligence (ODNI), which coordinates the various branches of the intelligence community, released a report that is the most comprehensive public accounting of post-Snowden reforms.

But how much has actually changed?

"It's kind of dizzying," said Elizabeth Goitein, co-director of the Brennan Center for Justice's program on liberty and national security, of the flurry of reports and announcements. "The volume of information, and the sheer number of developments make it hard to sort out what's significant."

She added: "From a big picture analysis, there's been a lot of developments without a whole lot of movement. ... These reforms just feel like gestures."

The release of the ODNI report may represent one of the biggest post-Snowden changes, according to privacy experts. It is the first of what's expected to be annual reviews of intelligence community programs.

"I think the most substantial changes that have occurred come in the area of transparency," said Mark Rumold, a senior attorney for the Electronic Frontier Foundation who has been tracking the government's disclosures. "I'm not satisfied, but things were so broken beforehand that any small change is an improvement."

FRONTLINE sifted through the various reports and recommendations to understand what the government has changed post-Snowden — and just how much is still exactly the same.

There Are Now "Appropriate Safeguards" for Personal Data—Unless It Conflicts with National Security

Obama's 2014 directive required the intelligence community to put in place "appropriate safeguards" for the personal information of people caught up in the surveillance dragnet. Most of those aren't specified. But the government has made one significant change.

For the first time, the personal information of non-U.S. citizens now can only be kept for five years — the same length as Americans' data, according to the ODNI report. If, within five years, agents haven't determined whether the information is important, it must be deleted — unless the DNI determines that there's a national security reason to keep it.

The policy means that the NSA is still allowed to hold on to any information it collects on anyone, whether it's relevant or not, for at least five years.

Still, Rumold said, that's a step forward. "It was basically the Wild West before the Snowden disclosures," he said. "The government was hanging onto anything related to non-U.S. persons and doing whatever they wanted. Now they've started to implement small changes around the margins. To give them credit, that is an improvement — but still not a particularly substantial change."

The Government Can Still Gather Data on Americans Without a Warrant

When the government collects foreigners' information, it inevitably scoops up Americans' communications, too. The government deems this "incidental" collection, but agents can still access and search this data without a warrant. Civil liberties experts, who call this "backdoor" collection, have raised concerns that such data could be used against Americans in court if authorities turned up evidence of a crime.

In fact, the president's review group recommended that authorities obtain a warrant to search this data. The ODNI has not made that change.

Under current policy as detailed in the ODNI report, data gathered this way on Americans can only be used against them in a criminal case "when appropriate." To the government, that means only when the information yields evidence related to national security offenses or other serious crimes including death, kidnapping, "substantial bodily harm," crimes against minors, destruction of critical infrastructure, transnational crimes, cyber security and human trafficking. The attorney general must also approve handing off the data.

Even so, privacy advocates, including Goitein, say that the provisions still violate the constitutional protections against search and seizure without a warrant for all crimes — even the serious ones. "It's a pretty bald-faced end-run around the Fourth Amendment," she said.

And while the ODNI said that the NSA and CIA have put in place new curbs on how much they collect — "minimization," in NSA-speak — Rumold said it doesn't seem to limit what is gathered by the FBI, which conducts the majority of searches for information on Americans. "The agencies that did get some restrictions placed on them do the least amount of U.S.-person querying of that data," Rumold said. As for the FBI: "It doesn't appear that their minimization procedures changed at all."

National Security Letters Now Expire—Unless the FBI Decides to Keep Them Open

National Security Letters allow the FBI to secretly compel companies, such as phone or internet service providers, financial institutions or even libraries, to turn over communications or other data on a specific person. The letters come with a gag order prohibiting the recipient from notifying the person in question, or even acknowledging they were given the document.

Now, the gag order expires after three years, the ODNI report said — unless the FBI writes a letter requesting the order remain in effect. Companies can still fight the order in court.

The move "doesn't fix the constitutional problem," Rumold said. "The constitutional problem is that there's a gag order when [a letter] is issued, without any judicial involvement or showing that there needs to be a gag. What they've done is shorten the indefinite unconstitutional gag to a three-year unconstitutional gag."

Bulk Collection of Telephone Metadata Is Still in Place

Obama said last year that he wanted to "end the Section 215 bulk metadata program as it currently exists."

That hasn't happened, despite recommendations to scrap the program by both the review group Obama set up in 2013, and the civil liberties oversight board. In its latest report, the board noted that the president could end the program "at any time, without Congressional involvement."

The president has curtailed the extent of the data gathered for each query. Instead of gathering all the data for people three "hops," or contacts, removed from the designated target, they now can collect only the numbers for two hops — although that's still a lot of phone numbers. Any query now also requires advanced approval from the secret court designed to evaluate such requests, the Foreign Intelligence Security Court.

But, Goitein said, "The NSA still collects all of this stuff and holds onto it."

The bulk collection authorization remains in place until the provision expires on June 1, 2015. After that, the program would need to be reauthorized by Congress. Section 215 was initially approved by Congress in 2001 as part of the Patriot Act, a law signed by President George W. Bush.

A new piece of legislation, the USA Freedom Act, sponsored by Rep. Jim Sensenbrenner (R-Wisc.), would end bulk collection under Section 215, allowing the government to gather data only on individuals after receiving court permission. The Obama administration backs the bill, but it's unclear how it will fare in the new Congress.

The Government Won't Say How It Handles NSA Employees Who Abuse Their Power

In 2013, *The Wall Street Journal* reported that some NSA employees misused their authority to search bulk data for personal information on significant others. The abuse happened so often it was nicknamed LOVEINT, after the intelligence community's practice of assigning nicknames to their intelligence gathering protocols. (The programs that collect phone and email records is known as SIGINT, for signals intelligence.)

Last week, Sen. Charles Grassley (R-Iowa) sent a letter to the Justice Department pointing out that he had asked for information back in 2013 about how it had handled reports of these alleged, unauthorized spying incidents. He's still waiting for a response.

The Government Still Spies on (Some) Foreign Leaders

One of the more damaging revelations amid the Snowden disclosures for the Obama administration was that the NSA had monitored the phones of 35 world leaders. On the list of numbers: the cell phone of close allies, including German Chancellor Angela Merkel. (The report, which appeared in *The Guardian*, also noted that the surveillance produced "little reportable intelligence.")

President Obama said that he hadn't been aware that was happening. And the administration has since pledged to remove Merkel — and several others it wouldn't name — from the list.

"The leaders of our close friends and allies deserve to know that if I want to know what they think about an issue I'll pick up the phone and call them rather than turning to surveillance," Obama said in a speech last year.

The ODNI now has a procedure in place to ensure at the very least high-level U.S. officials are aware of any monitoring of top foreign officials. But it also leaves the door open to begin — or continue — gathering information from anyone in the interest of national security.

"In the annals of international spying, I don't think it changes much, but at least the president won't be able to say that he wasn't aware that it was going on," Rumold said.

> "He collected an apparently unknowable amount of information (unknowable to both him and the NSA) and dumped it on the doorsteps of largely foreign newspapers."

Yes, Edward Snowden Is a Traitor

Zachary Keck

The previous viewpoint focused on the effects of Edward Snowden's revelations about the NSA spying program. In this viewpoint, Zachary Keck takes up the question of Snowden's motives and responsibility. Ultimately, the question is: were Snowden's actions traitorous? In this viewpoint, Keck argues that they were. The NSA works to protect the safety of American citizens, and Snowden's actions endangered this mission. Zachary Keck is a foreign policy expert, defenses analyst, and former staffer on the U.S. House Foreign Affairs Committee. His expertise is in nuclear weapons issues and defense.

As you read, consider the following questions:

1. According to Keck, how were Snowden's actions different from what a true whistleblower would have done?
2. How did Snowden justify not selectively releasing the information, according to Keck?

"Yes, Edward Snowden Is a Traitor," by Zachary Keck, Diplomat Media, Inc., December 21, 2013. Reprinted by permission.

3. Does Keck think it's significant that Snowden fled first to China, then to Russia? Why or why not?

When the Edward Snowden story first burst on the scene early this year, one of the central debates that ensued was whether Snowden should be considered a whistleblower or a traitor. In the months since, this debate has largely faded from the conversation.

The events of this week are starting to revive that debate. Proof enough of this was a conversation this week on *MSNBC*'s Morning Joe, a sort of bellwether of Inside the Beltway thinking. In response to a federal judge ruling that the National Security Agency's collection of telephone metadata was unconstitutional, Joe Scarborough, the former Florida Congressman who hosts Morning Joe, asked whether this made Snowden a whistleblower.

While claiming that he "didn't know the definition of whistleblower," Scarborough suggested that he believed Snowden might be one in light of the fact that the federal judge said the NSA's actions would be deeply offensive to James Madison, the father of the U.S. constitution. John Heileman, one half of the unofficial biographers of recent U.S. presidential elections, agreed, saying the court's ruling "vindicated" Snowden's action.

I disagree and in fact would argue that at this point it is beyond dispute that Snowden is a traitor. Full disclosure: I always felt that Snowden was a traitor. This is not because I disagreed with his view that the NSA is out of control. Given the level of threat presented by terrorism today, I too am deeply worried by the extent the NSA goes to prevent these hypothetical attacks. One cannot help but be concerned about what America's fate should a serious security threat materialize.

The reason why I believed from the beginning that Snowden was a traitor was not because of the information he had been leaking but the manner in which he had done it. In my view, a true whistleblower would have first pursued legal avenues for reining in the NSA, such as seeking out sympathetic members of Congress. The American people, after all, elect people to serve in

Should the Government Spy on Its Own Citizens?

Congress specifically for the purpose of representing their interests on important matters of state.

Additionally, in my view, a true patriotic whistleblower believes in his or her cause enough to be willing to accept the punishment their disclosures bring. If they truly believe in the righteousness of their cause, they'll be confident enough that the American people will ultimately come to appreciate their actions and they'll be pardoned. Snowden's flight to Hong Kong and then Moscow showed he wasn't willing to suffer the consequences for his actions, calling into question how much he believed in his cause.

This being said, while I personally felt this all made him a traitor, in the early days of the Snowden story I felt that there could a legitimate debate over whether he was a whistleblower or not. After all, while fleeing abroad certainly made Snowden a coward, it didn't necessarily preclude him from being a whistleblower. The information he disclosed wasn't necessarily any less important to restoring Americans' liberty because of his personal shortcomings.

It has long since become apparent that Snowden should be viewed as a traitor, however. The main reason that Snowden cannot be seen as a whistleblower is the careless ways in which he collected and leaked information, which have only become fully apparent after the first month or so of the Snowden story breaking. Had Snowden been a whistleblower interested in protecting the American constitution, he would have carefully collected information documenting NSA overreach in spying on Americans. Only that would have been given to the journalists and newspapers Snowden contacted.

Instead, he collected an apparently unknowable amount of information (unknowable to both him and the NSA) and dumped it on the doorsteps of largely foreign newspapers. As he no doubt fully understood, most of these documents contained information pertaining to how the NSA collected intelligence on legitimate foreign targets, not Americans whatsoever.

Snowden of course would defend himself by pointing out that he hasn't chosen what was published from his stolen documents. Indeed, he has quite self-righteously said that he believed he was too biased to determine what information it was in the public interest to publish. That is why, Snowden has claimed, he gave it to responsible journalists and editors to decide on which documents needed to be kept secret, and which the public should know about.

While all this sounds very noble it conveniently ignores the fact that society has not appointed journalists or newspaper editors to decide these matters, nor are they qualified to do so. In fact, journalists and editors ultimately have a different immediate interest than the American public; namely, the former are interested first and foremost in selling newspapers, not protecting U.S. national security. They may sometimes withhold information at the government's request, but in general their preference is heavily weighted towards publishing information that sells papers.

This has been fully on display in the case of Snowden's leaks. Although I haven't been keeping a precise scorecard, it seems to me that the overwhelming majority of the stories that have been published from the Snowden documents are about U.S. spying on foreign nations, not its domestic operations. Americans' rights are not at risk when the NSA taps the phones of foreign leaders. As such, leaking these documents were not the actions of a patriotic whistleblower.

In fact, as others have pointed out, information from the Snowden documents has been published in a manner that seemingly seeks to do as much harm to U.S. alliances across the world as possible. Meanwhile, Snowden seeking refuge in first China and then Russia nearly guarantees that the governments in these countries have gained a treasure trove of valuable information on NSA operations against their countries.

Stealing classified information to systematically undermine U.S. alliances across the world, while aiding U.S. adversaries, is practically the definition of treason. Snowden couldn't help but know that his actions would lead to these outcomes. And for that reason it is beyond dispute that Snowden, regardless of whether or not some of his disclosures had any merit, has betrayed the United States and his fellow citizens. Nothing from this week or in the future will change this fact.

VIEWPOINT 3

> "With the latest court document released by the ODNI, it is clear that the 'general warrant' model ... is nothing but a cover for the ongoing violation of the basic rights guaranteed by the Fourth Amendment ..."

Surveillance Programs Violate the U.S. Constitution

Kevin Reed

In this viewpoint, Kevin Reed argues that despite efforts to bring it into line with the law, the court-approved surveillance program violates the Fourth Amendment of the U.S. Constitution, the amendment that guarantees protection against unreasonable search and seizure. This is because the program allows the FBI to conduct searches of emails and other electronic communications from U.S. citizens and non-citizens without a warrant. Kevin Reed is a writer for the World Socialist Web Site and a member of the Socialist Equality Party.

As you read, consider the following questions:

1. What examples does Reed give of the FBI conducting data searches of U.S. citizens? Why is this not covered by FISA laws?

"Secret US court approved surveillance program despite continuing FBI constitutional violations," by Kevin Reed, World Socialist Web Site, April 27, 2021. Reprinted by permission.

2. What was the original purpose of the FISA law?
3. Reed quotes Edward Snowden commenting that the court was concerned only with misuse of FISA by the FBI. What do Snowden and Reed see as the larger problem?

The FBI has repeatedly violated the law in conducting warrantless searches of email messages and other electronic communications of US citizens, according to a November 2020 certification report from the court established to oversee the surveillance program.

The Office of the Director of National Intelligence (ODNI), Avril Haynes, who was appointed by President Joe Biden and sworn in on January 21, released the redacted certification report from the Foreign Intelligence Surveillance Court (FISC) to the public on Monday. Significantly, while pointing to "widespread violations" by the FBI, FISC presiding judge James E. Boasberg approved the continuation of the program for the second year in a row.

In his 67-page ruling, Judge Boasberg recounts instances when FBI agents searched the electronic information of US citizens without getting the appropriate FISA court authorizations. However, he wrote, "While the court is concerned about the apparent widespread violations of the querying standard, it lacks sufficient information at this time to assess the adequacy of the FBI system changes and training, post-implementation."

For example, the judge's report found that the FBI made 40 secret queries and collected data not about foreigners—the purported purpose of the FISA law—but about American citizens for investigations of "healthcare fraud, transnational organized crime, violent gangs, domestic terrorism involving racially motivated violent extremists, as well as investigations connected to public corruption and bribery."

In another instance, Judge Boasberg reports that an FBI specialist conducting "background investigations" made 124 queries of raw NSA data using the names of individuals who were participating in an FBI "Citizens Academy," a program to increase awareness of the bureau's role in the community; those who needed to enter a field office to perform a service such as repairs; and others who were seeking to report tips or crimes.

If these are the violations being admitted by the court, the public has a right to know how many others of a more serious, criminal and deadly character have taken place. Clearly, the FISA court report—released nearly six months after it was submitted—is just the tip of the FBI warrantless surveillance iceberg.

The previous reports from 2017–2019 showed similar violations by the FBI, with tens of thousands of US citizens having their email and phone call data searched without warrants or

Edward Snowden: Traitor or Hero?

In 2013, computer expert and former CIA systems administrator, Edward Snowden released confidential government documents to the press about the existence of government surveillance programs. According to many legal experts, and the U.S. government, his actions violated the Espionage Act of 1917, which identified the leak of state secrets as an act of treason. Yet despite the fact that he broke the law, Snowden argued that he had a moral obligation to act. He gave a justification for his "whistleblowing" by stating that he had a duty "to inform the public as to that which is done in their name and that which is done against them." According to Snowden, the government's violation of privacy had to be exposed regardless of legality.

Many agreed with Snowden. Jesselyn Radack of the Government Accountability Project defended his actions as ethical, arguing that he acted from a sense of public good. Radack said:

Snowden may have violated a secrecy agreement, which is not a loyalty oath but a contract, and a less important one than the social contract a democracy has with its citizenry.

approval by a FISA court. As NSA whistleblower Edward Snowden tweeted following the revelations last year, "The worst part? The government argues the existence of a warrantless, internet-scale mass surveillance program isn't the problem, merely the lawless way the FBI uses it against Americans, [because] 'of course' the other 93–97% of the human population have no rights."

One of the factors cited by the judge for approving the program again was the fact that the coronavirus pandemic limited the government's ability to adequately monitor compliance with rules set up in a 2018 renewal of the FISA law. Therefore, the court concluded that "the FBI's querying and minimization procedures meet statutory and Fourth Amendment requirements."

> Others argued that even if he was legally culpable, he was not ethically culpable because the law itself was unjust and unconstitutional.
> The Attorney General of the United States, Eric Holder, did not find Snowden's rationale convincing. Holder stated:
>
> He broke the law. He caused harm to our national security and I think that he has to be held accountable for his actions.
>
> Journalists were conflicted about the ethical implications of Snowden's actions. The editorial board of *The New York Times* stated, "He may have committed a crime…but he has done his country a great service." In an Op-ed in the same newspaper, Ed Morrissey argued that Snowden was not a hero, but a criminal: "by leaking information about the behavior rather than reporting it through legal channels, Snowden chose to break the law." According to Morrissey, Snowden should be prosecuted for his actions, arguing that his actions broke a law "intended to keep legitimate national-security data and assets safe from our enemies; it is intended to keep Americans safe."
>
> "Edward Snowden: Traitor or Hero?," Ethics Unwrapped, McCombs School of Business – The University of Texas at Austin.

Meanwhile, the report summarizes and "clarifies" a convoluted set of procedures for the National Security Agency (NSA), Central Intelligence Agency (CIA) and National Counterterrorism Center (NCTC) to work with the FBI in conducting domestic investigations such that "terrorists" and "terrorism networks" are adequately "targeted" and the monitoring of their electronic communications is sufficiently "minimized" and "segregated" from that of US citizens.

Behind the façade of rules and procedures that have been repeatedly ignored by the FBI is the language of Section 702 of the FISA Act of 1978. Originally passed in response to the Nixon administration's use of federal resources and law enforcement agencies to illegally spy on political organizations and individuals within the US, the purpose of FISA was to permit warrantless surveillance of foreigners that may include the communications of US citizens under very narrow circumstances that were specifically approved by a secret FISA court.

After the attacks of September 11, 2001, the administration of George W. Bush asserted that the executive powers of the president could override the FISA warrant requirement. At that time, the NSA began gathering the electronic communications of everyone on the planet—as revealed in 2013 by the former intelligence analyst and whistleblower Edward Snowden—in complete violation of the US Constitution. In 2008, Congress legalized the practice, enacting Section 702 of the FISA Amendments Act.

In 2018, Section 702 was amended to require an annual review by the FISA court of the procedures limiting how and when analysts may query the repository for information about Americans and how well the FBI is following these rules.

As explained by the *New York Times*, Section 702 "authorizes the government to gather, without warrants, the phone calls and internet messages of noncitizens abroad with assistance from American companies, like Google and AT&T—even when the foreign target is communicating with an American, raising the question of what the rules should be for Americans' messages that get swept in.

"The surveillance is carried out by the National Security Agency, but three other entities—the CIA, the National Counterterrorism Center and the FBI—also receive access to streams of 'raw' messages intercepted without a warrant for their analysts to use. Of those, the FBI is the only one that also has a law enforcement mission, heightening the stakes.

"The FBI receives only a small portion of the messages that the National Security Agency vacuums up: The bureau gets copies of intercepts to and from targets who are deemed relevant to a full and active FBI national security investigation. Presently, that amounts to about 3.6 percent of the National Security Agency's targets, a senior FBI official told reporters in a news briefing on Monday."

In other words, the US government has never stopped gathering all of the electronic communications of the entire world and it is continuing to do so, even in the aftermath of the Snowden revelations and the enactment of supposed reforms and restrictions by Congress.

The only thing that has changed is the Section 702 requirement that the FBI must get FISA court approval to query the data of US citizens, something that has been established for years now that the FBI does not do. Meanwhile, all of the data gathering and monitoring activity by the NSA exposed by Snowden continues and is expanding, and none of it is "minimized" or "segregated" in the slightest.

Speaking to the *Washington Post*, Julian Sanchez, a senior fellow at the Cato Institute, said, "We can continue playing compliance whack-a-mole, but at this point, it's reasonable to ask whether this sort of large-scale collection on a 'general warrant' model is inherently prone to these problems in a way that resists robust and timely oversight."

With the latest court document released by the ODNI, it is clear that the "general warrant" model—regardless of which party controls the White House or the Congress—is nothing but a cover for the ongoing violation of the basic rights guaranteed by the Fourth Amendment to the US Constitution against unreasonable searches and seizures.

VIEWPOINT 4

> "They really did shift from individual warrants to approving whole programs and whole programs that really went beyond, is this person a spy to let's look at this whole network and see maybe if there is something that indicates that a spy might be there."

The FISA Court Invades the Privacy of Americans Without Oversight

Cindy Cohn, Danny O'Brien, and Julian Sanchez

In the previous viewpoint, the author argued that the warrantless surveillance authorized by Section 702 of the Foreign Intelligence Surveillance Act of 1978 (FISA) is unconstitutional. In this excerpted viewpoint, which is a transcript of a podcast by the Electronic Frontier Foundation (EFF), the authors explain what the FISA Court is, how it came to have this much power, and how FISA changed over the years. While the FISA Court has always been secret, in the past the court only issued individual warrants to intelligence agencies for spies. In the post-9/11 era, however, the court has started allowing mass surveillance and the collection of electronic metadata. Changes in technology that have occurred since FISA was originally passed in 1978 have also contributed to these increased powers. Danny

"Podcast Episode: The Secret Court Approving Secret Surveillance," by Cindy Cohn, Danny O'Brien, and Julian Sanchez, Electronic Frontier Foundation, November 12, 2020, https://www.eff.org/deeplinks/2020/11/secret-court-approving-secret-surveillance. Licensed under CC BY 4.0 International.

O'Brien is an EFF special advisor and a senior fellow at the Filecoin Foundation and the Filecoin Foundation for the Decentralized Web. Cindy Cohn is a lawyer and executive director of EFF. Julian Sanchez is a writer and former senior fellow at the Cato Institute.

As you read, consider the following questions:

1. According to Sanchez, what is the rationale behind having a secret court to handle intelligence warrants?
2. According to Sanchez, how has "the shift toward more programmatic sorts of surveillance" changed how the FISA Court operates?
3. What role have changes in technology played in the kinds of data that the FISA Court allows intelligence agencies to collect?

Cindy Cohn: Our topic today is the Foreign Intelligence Surveillance Court, which is also called the FISC or the FISA Court. The judges who sit on this court are hand picked by the chief justice of the United States Supreme Court, that's currently Justice Roberts. The FISA Court meets in secret and has a limited public docket and until recently it had almost no public records of its decisions. In fact, the very first case on the FISC docket was an EFF transparency case that ended up getting referred to the FISC. But this where almost all of the key decisions about the legality about America's mass Internet spying projects have been made and what that means is pretty much everybody in the United States is affected by the secret court's decisions despite having no influence over it and no input into it and no way to hold the court accountable if it gets things wrong.

Danny O'Brien: Joining us now to discuss just what an anomaly an American and global injustice the secret FISA Court is, and how we could do better is Julian Sanchez, the Cato Institute's specialist in surveillance legal policy. Before joining Cato, Julian served as the Washington editor for Ars Technica where he covered surveillance, intellectual property and telecom policy. He has also worked as a writer for the Economist blog, Democracy in America and is an editor for Reason Magazine where he remains a contributing editor. He's also on Twitter as Normative and that's one of my favorite follow there.

Julian, welcome to the podcast. We are so happy to have you hear today.

Julian Sanchez: Thanks for having me on.

[…]

Cindy Cohn: Why do we have a FISA Court? Where is it? I've talked a little about who is on it, but where does this idea come from?

Julian Sanchez: This grows out of the Foreign Intelligence Surveillance Act of 1978 that was passed in response to disclosures of a dizzying array of abuses of surveillance authority and their power more generally by the FBI especially, but the American intelligence community in general. For decades, oversimplifying a bit, effectively wire tapping had been initially just illegal period and then very tightly constrained and the FBI had essentially decided those rules can't possibly really apply to us and so FISA, for the first time, created an intelligence specific framework for doing electronic surveillance. The idea of having a separate court for this, I think, grew out of a number of factors.

One is the sense that there was this need for extreme secrecy where you were dealing with potentially people with foreign state backing who were not necessarily going to be sticking around for criminal prosecution. And when you're talking about intelligence gathering, criminal prosecution isn't necessarily the point. And so this is an activity that is not really designed to yield criminal cases. You don't really want the methods ever disclosed. You're dealing with adversaries who have the capability to potentially plant people in ordinary courts, that's where you're discussing interests, sources, and methods in your intelligence so there was a sense that it would be better to have a separate, extra secure court. And also that you might not want to have to explain all this both highly sensitive and potentially quite complicated intelligence practices and information to whatever random magistrate judge happened to be on the roster in the jurisdiction where you were looking.

And also that the nature of intelligence surveillance is quite different in so far as, again, you're not necessarily looking at someone who has committed a crime, you think someone is working on behalf of a foreign power and trying to gather intelligence for them or engage in clandestine intelligence activities. But you don't necessarily have a specific crime you think has been committed. Your purpose in gathering intelligence is not to prosecute crimes. These are the cluster of reasons around the formation of a separate court for that purpose and it originally consisted of seven federal circuit judges, now it's 11 after the USA Patriot Act increased the number and so they continue serving on their regular courts and then, in effect, take turns in rotation sitting for a week and hearing applications from the Justice Department and the FBI to conduct electronic surveillance.

Cindy Cohn: The court started out as one thing, this idea of individual secret warrants for spies basically, but it's really changed in the past decade. Can you walk us through how those shifts happened and why?

Julian Sanchez: And of course to the extent that older FISA Court opinions are not available. The first ever published opinion of FISA Court was in 2002 and it was quite a few years before we got a second. Now quite a number of more recent ones are public, but we still have to speculate about the earlier history of the court, but veterans of the court, that is retired FISC judges have effectively confirmed that, in its early years the FISA Court was primarily about assessing the adequacy of individual warrant applications. It was just a bread and butter magistrate judge usually almost scut work. Okay, have you made the showing that there is probable cause to believe that the target of the surveillance is an agent of a foreign power. You have, you haven't. In 99.9% of cases, it was, you have and they took a pass on that individual warrant and as we get to the, in particular, the post-9/11 era and you're dealing with questions of trying to, one, often figure out who an unknown target is. You might have someone who's using a particular email address or other account that you don't otherwise necessarily have an identity.

You're potentially trying to sift through a lot of data to figure out who your target is or which data pertains to the people you're interested in. There is a shift toward more programmatic sorts of surveillance and so the court increasingly is not passing on the question of have you established a probable cause showing with respect to "bad guy X" but rather does the law, does a statute written to deal with pre-Internet communications technology permit you to do the surveillance you're contemplating and in particular, might it allow you to gather information in ways that go beyond just targeting a particular facility, a particular phone line, that is the home phone of a particular known target. And so it ended up building this kind of secret body of precedent around what kinds of programs for Internet type network surveillance were permissible under a statute that was not written with that in mind.

Cindy Cohn: They really did shift from individual warrants to approving whole programs and whole programs that really went beyond, is this person a spy to let's look at this whole network and see maybe if there is something that indicates that a spy might be there. It really flips the kind of basis way that we think about investigations. From my perspective, obviously, I've been litigating this in the courts for a long time so it kind of flipped the whole thing on its head.

Julian Sanchez: And so we know, for example, maybe I should give some maybe more concrete examples. We know there was a bulk telephony metadata program under one FISA authority that actually was sort of the second case of this kind the FISA Court had to consider. There was an earlier question presented by a program that used what was called the pen trap authority, pen register trap and trace authority, which is, in the traditional phone context, this is about essentially real-time metadata surveillance. Meaning let's say there's a particular phone number that we think is up to no good, maybe we don't have a full blown probable cause wiretap order for that number yet, but we want to know who this target is calling and whose calling that target.

A pen register trap and trace order lets you get realtime data about what calls are happening to and from that number and who they are from and how long the call lasts and in the Internet era the question is, what kind of realtime metadata does that let you get and when the statute talks about a facility at which this information collection is directed, traditionally that meant a phone number is the facility, but in the Internet era, you had questions like, because the standard for this kind of trap is because you're not getting full blown, in theory, you're getting the full content, the full email, the full phone conversation. You can get one of these pen trap orders under Section 214 of the USA Patriot Act with a lot less than probable cause.

The question is, we're talking about regular phones anymore, we're talking about Internet accounts and IP addresses and server. What can a facility be? Can we say, we want all the metadata and the realtime transactional information for a particular server and all the traffic coming to and from that? So we're not just talking about one individual phone line or maybe even a corporate phone line used by a number of people, but facilities that may be handling millions of peoples traffic, or at least tens of thousands of peoples traffic. The court, I don't think that is an opinion that is public in full at this point, but essentially said, at least with respect to international communications, we're going to be pretty permissive about what you can collect.

Danny O'Brien: This is the other shift that I see, which is that not only is FISA not dealing with regular phones anymore, but it's dealing with these big servers with millions of people, but also the sort of target has changed too, partly because we're not really talking about agents of a foreign power, we're not talking about spy versus spy. It became much more dissolved than that. It's like we're talking about random stochastic terrorists who you don't necessarily know who they are. But also, this switch between "we can do foreign surveillance because we're targeting foreign powers and their spies", to "we're just surveilling foreigners", like they don't have rights under this court. So the question is, how do we scoop out this data and separate the stuff that legally we are concerned about, which is US citizens communications, but everything else is kind of fair game. And then we have a secret court that doesn't even have any kind of representation of US citizens interests, but also making this kind of human rights and foreign policy decision too.

Julian Sanchez: The debate around the authorities that the FISA Court oversees has been very, US citizens-centric, so you can watch tapes from CSPAN where a lot of defenders are saying, "look, as long as they are targeting foreigners, who cares if they don't have constitutional rights". Some of us think, people are human and have human rights even if they had the poor taste to be born somewhere other than the United States and so this is perhaps not something we should entirely shrug off. But also that there's this interesting shift from the idea that you should be concerned if the communications of an American with Fourth Amendment rights are surveilled too. The idea that really what's significant in terms of encroaching on peoples' rights is who is targeted. And for practical reasons, of course, you understand why this would be the focus because you cannot in advance know whose communications you will intercept when you target somebody. You know who you're going to target, but you have no idea who they might talk to. That's the point in part of doing the surveillance.

But if you look at the text of the Fourth Amendment, it doesn't say the "right of the people against being targeted shall not be violated". It says, "the right of the people to be secure in their persons and houses" and papers or the digital equivalent thereof. And in a sense, the fundamental Fourth Amendment concern was, at the time, were the general warrants, with the idea of these sort of open-ended authorizations to search, that did not target anyone. From the perspective of the people who signed off on the Fourth Amendment, it was not a mitigating consideration to say, don't worry if your communications are collected, you weren't the target. The thing they found most egregious, the thing they thought was the most defensive abuse was surveillance that did not have a particular target that made it open to anyone to be swept into the dragnet.

[...]

VIEWPOINT

> "Critics warned that the government's new anti-terrorism tools were eroding civil liberties, while the American Muslim community felt it was all too often the target of an overzealous FBI."

After 9/11, Authorities Toe the Line Between Protecting Lives and Protecting Rights

Ryan Lucas

Most of the arguments made so far in this chapter have been based, in one way or another, on the need to protect the United States from terrorism, and whether that does or does not require violating some rights along the way. In this viewpoint, Ryan Lucas explains the challenges of protecting the country from an ever-changing threat and how that resulted in an erosion of civil liberties. The development of the digital world in the post-9/11 era has provided terrorists—including domestic terrorists—new tools for orchestrating attacks, which has led to a need for greater digital surveillance. Ryan Lucas is a correspondent for National Public Radio.

©2021 National Public Radio, Inc. NPR news report titled "The World Has Changed Since 9/11, And So Has America's Fight Against Terrorism" by Ryan Lucas was originally published on npr.org on September 10, 2021, and is used with the permission of NPR. Any unauthorized duplication is strictly prohibited.

Espionage and Intelligence

As you read, consider the following questions:

1. What steps did the U.S. government take in the immediate aftermath of 9/11, according to this viewpoint?
2. How did the FBI change in response to 9/11?
3. How did fighting terrorism erode civil liberties, according to Lucas? Has domestic terrorism complicated the approach?

In the fall of 2001, Aaron Zebley was a 31-year-old FBI agent in New York. He had just transferred to a criminal squad after working counterterrorism cases for years.

His first day in the new job was Sept. 11.

"I was literally cleaning the desk, I was like wiping the desk when Flight 11 hit the north tower, and it shook our building," he said. "And I was like, what the heck was that? And later that day, I was transferred back to counterterrorism."

It was a natural move for Zebley. He'd spent the previous three years investigating al-Qaida's bombings of U.S. embassies in Kenya and Tanzania. And he became a core member of the FBI team leading the investigation into the 9/11 attacks.

It quickly became clear that al-Qaida was responsible.

The hijackers had trained at the group's camps in Afghanistan. They received money and instructions from its leadership. And ultimately, they were sent to the U.S. to carry out al-Qaida's "planes operation."

As the nation mourned the nearly 3,000 people who were killed on 9/11, the George W. Bush administration frantically tried to find its footing and prevent what many feared would be a second wave of attacks.

President Bush ordered members of his administration, including top counterterrorism official Richard Clarke, to imagine what the next attack could look like and take steps to prevent it.

"We had so many vulnerabilities in this country," Clarke said.

At the time, officials were worried that al-Qaida could use chemical weapons or radioactive materials, Clarke said, or that the group would target intercity trains or subway systems.

"We had a very long list of things, systems, that were vulnerable because no one in the United States had seriously considered security from terrorist attacks," he said.

That, of course, quickly changed.

Security became paramount.

And over the next two decades, the federal government poured money and resources — some of it, critics say, to no good use — into protecting the U.S. from another terrorist attack, even as the nature of that threat continuously evolved.

The Response to Keeping the U.S. Secure Takes Shape

The government built out a massive infrastructure, including creating the Department of Homeland Security, all in the name of protecting against terrorist attacks.

The Bush administration also empowered the FBI and its partners at the CIA, National Security Agency and the Pentagon to take the fight to al-Qaida.

The military invaded Afghanistan, which had been a haven for the group. The CIA hunted down al-Qaida operatives around the world and tortured many of them in secret prisons.

The Bush administration also launched its ill-fated war in Iraq, which unleashed two decades of bloodletting, shook the Middle East and spawned another generation of terrorists.

On the homefront, FBI Director Robert Mueller shifted some 2,000 agents to counterterrorism work as he tried to transform the FBI from a crime-fighting first organization into a more intelligence-driven one that prioritized combating terrorism and preventing the next attack.

Part of that involved centralizing the bureau's international terrorism investigations at headquarters and making counterterrorism the FBI's top priority.

Chuck Rosenberg, who served as a top aide to Mueller in those early years, said the changes Mueller imposed amounted to a paradigm shift for the bureau.

"Mueller, God bless him, couldn't be all that patient about it," Rosenberg said. "It couldn't happen at a normal pace of a traditional cultural change. It had to happen yesterday."

It had to happen "yesterday" because al-Qaida was still plotting. Overseas, its operatives carried out horrific bombings in Bali, Madrid, London and elsewhere.

In the U.S., al-Qaida operative Richard Reid was arrested in December 2001 after trying to blow up a trans-Atlantic flight with a bomb hidden in his shoe. More plots were foiled in the ensuing years, including one targeting the Brooklyn Bridge.

Over time, the FBI and its partners better understood al-Qaida, its hierarchical structure, and how to unravel the various threads of a plot.

That stemmed to large degree, Zebley says, from the U.S. getting better at pulling together various threads of intelligence and by upping the operational tempo.

"If you have a little thread that could potentially tell you about a terrorist plot, not only were we much better at integrating the intelligence, but we did it at a pace that was tenfold what we were doing before," he said.

But critics warned that the government's new anti-terrorism tools were eroding civil liberties, while the American Muslim community felt it was all too often the target of an overzealous FBI.

The Digital World Helps Transform Terrorism

By the early days of the Obama administration, the U.S. had to a large extent hardened the homeland against 9/11-style plots. But the terrorism landscape was evolving.

At that time, Zebley was serving as a senior aide to Mueller. Each morning, he would sit in on the FBI director's daily threat briefing.

"I was thinking about al-Qaida for years leading up until that moment," he said. "And now I'm sitting in these morning threat briefings and I'm seeing al-Qaida in the Arabian Peninsula, al-Qaida in the Islamic Maghreb in North Africa, al-Shabab. ... One of my first thoughts was 'the map looks very different to me now.'"

Ultimately, AQAP — al-Qaida's branch based in Yemen — emerged as a significant threat to the U.S. homeland.

That became clear in November 2009 when U.S. Army Maj. Nidal Hasan shot and killed 13 people at Fort Hood, Texas. A month later, on Christmas Day, a young Nigerian man tried to blow up a passenger jet over Detroit with a bomb hidden in his underwear.

It quickly emerged that both men had been in contact with a senior AQAP figure, an American-born Yemeni cleric named Anwar al-Awlaki.

"My sense when I first heard about him was 'well, he's some charismatic guy, born in the U.S., fluent English speaker and all that. But how big a threat could he be?" said John Pistole, who served as the No. 2 official at the FBI from 2004 until 2010 when he left to lead the Transportation Security Administration.

"I think I failed to recognize and appreciate his ability to influence others to action."

Awlaki used the internet to spread his calls for violence against America, and his lectures and ideas influenced attacks in several countries. Awlaki was killed in a U.S. drone strike in 2011, a move that proved controversial because he was an American citizen.

A few years later, a different terrorist group emerged from the cauldron of Syria and Iraq — the Islamic State, or ISIS, a group that would build on Awlaki's savvy use of the digital world.

"When ISIS came onto the scene, particularly that summer of 2014, with the beheadings and the prolific use of social media, it was off the charts," said Mary McCord, who was a senior national security official at the Justice Department at the time.

Like al-Qaida more than a decade before, ISIS used its stronghold to plan operations abroad, such as the coordinated attacks in 2015 that killed 130 people in Paris. But it also used social media platforms such as Twitter and Telegram to pump out slickly produced propaganda videos.

"They deployed technology in a much more sophisticated way than we had seen with most other foreign terrorist organizations," McCord said.

ISIS produced materials featuring idyllic scenes of life in the caliphate to entice people to move there. At the same time, the group pushed out a torrent of videos showing horrendous violence that sought to instill fear in ISIS' enemies and to inspire the militants' sympathizers in Europe and the U.S. to conduct attacks where they were.

"The threat was much more horizontal. It was harder to corral," said Chuck Rosenberg, who served as FBI Director James Comey's chief of staff.

People inspired by ISIS could go from watching the group's videos to action relatively quickly without setting off alarms.

"It was clear too that there were going to be attacks we just couldn't stop. Things that went from left of boom to right of boom very quickly. People were more discreet, the thing we used to refer to as lone wolves," Rosenberg said. "A lot of bad things could happen, maybe on a smaller scale, but a lot of bad things could happen more quickly."

Bad Things Did Happen

Europe was hit by a series of deadly one-off attacks. In the U.S., a gunman killed 49 people at the Pulse nightclub in Orlando, Fla., in 2016. A year later, a man used a truck to plow through a group of cyclists and pedestrians in Manhattan, killing eight people. Both men had been watching ISIS propaganda.

The group's allure waned after a global coalition led by the U.S. managed to retake all the territory that ISIS once claimed.

By then, America's most lethal terror threat already stemmed not from foreign terror groups, but from the country's own domestic extremists.

For nearly two decades, the FBI had prioritized the fight against international terrorists. But in early 2020, FBI Director Christopher Wray said that had changed.

"We elevated to the top-level priority racially motivated violent extremism so it's on the same footing in terms of our national threat banding as ISISI and homegrown violent extremism," he testified before Congress.

The move came in the wake of a series of high-profile attacks by people espousing white supremacist views in Charlottesville, Va., Pittsburgh, Pa., Poway, Calif., and El Paso, Texas.

At the same time, anti-government extremist groups and conspiracy theories like QAnon were attracting more adherents.

Those various movements converged in Washington, D.C., on Jan. 6, 2021, in the storming of the U.S. Capitol as Congress was certifying Joe Biden's presidential win.

The FBI has since launched a massive investigation into the assault, and Wray has bluntly described the Capitol riot as "domestic terrorism."

McCord, who is now the executive director at the Institute for Constitutional Advocacy and Protection at the Georgetown University Law Center, says domestic extremist groups are using many of the same tools that foreign groups have for years.

"You see that in the use of social media for the same kind of things: to recruit, to propagandize, to plot, and to fundraise," she said.

The Capitol riot has put a spotlight on far-right extremism in a way the issue has never received in the past two decades, including in the media and the highest levels of the U.S. government.

President Biden, for one, has called political extremism and domestic terrorism a looming threat to the country that must be defeated, and he has made combating the threat a priority for his administration.

Periodical and Internet Sources Bibliography

The following articles have been selected to supplement the diverse views presented in this chapter.

Spencer Ackerman, "The FBI Is Back to Its Old Habits: Illegally Spying on Protesters," the *Nation*, June 9, 2023. https://www.thenation.com/article/society/fisa-section-702-fbi-surveillance/.

Dell Cameron, "The US Is Openly Stockpiling Dirt on All Its Citizens," *Wired*, June 12, 2023. https://www.wired.com/story/odni-commercially-available-information-report/.

Karoun Demirjian and Charlie Savage, "House Plan to Vote on Extension of Disputed Surveillance Law Collapses," *New York Times*, December 11, 2023. https://www.nytimes.com/2023/12/11/us/politics/house-fisa-surveillance-bill.html.

Elizabeth Goitein, "How the CIA Is Acting Outside the Law to Spy on Americans," Brennan Center for Justice, February 15, 2022. https://www.brennancenter.org/our-work/analysis-opinion/how-cia-acting-outside-law-spy-americans.

Ewen MacAskill, "'No Regrets,' Says Edward Snowden, After 10 Years in Exile," the *Guardian*, June 8, 2023. https://www.theguardian.com/us-news/2023/jun/08/no-regrets-says-edward-snowden-after-10-years-in-exile.

Branko Marcetic, "The CIA Is Still Spying on American Citizens and Lying About It," *Jacobin*, February 14, 2022. https://jacobin.com/2022/02/cia-spying-domestic-surveillance-program-data-collection.

Nomaan Merchant and Hannah Fingerhut, "Democrats and Republicans Are Skeptical of US Spying Practices, an AP-NORC Poll Finds," Associated Press, June 8, 2023. https://apnews.com/article/intelligence-section-702-apnorc-poll-4ef1e9f300395d0d7cda5b86cf7d5785.

Sara Morrison, "The US Government Is Buying Your Data to Spy on You," *Vox*, June 16, 2023. https://www.vox.com/technology/2023/6/16/23762403/data-odni-report-wyden.

Ed Pilkington, "'Panic Made Us Vulnerable': How 9/11 Made the US Surveillance State – and the Americans Who Fought Back," the

Guardian, September 4, 2021. https://www.theguardian.com/world/2021/sep/04/surveillance-state-september-11-panic-made-us-vulnerable.

Raphael Satter, "U.S. Court: Mass Surveillance Program Exposed by Snowden Was Illegal," Reuters, September 3, 2020. https://www.reuters.com/article/idUSKBN25T3CJ/.

Dina Temple-Raston, "Deception Has Changed in the Digital Era, and Spies Are Adapting," *Washington Post*, March 18, 2022. https://www.washingtonpost.com/outlook/2022/03/18/deception-has-changed-digital-era-spies-are-adapting/.

CHAPTER 4

Should Corporations Be Allowed to Spy on Private Citizens?

Chapter Preface

As the previous chapter suggests, there was a huge outcry when it came to light that the U.S. government had been spying on its own citizens. However, governments aren't the only ones who spy on private citizens. Corporations do it, too. And they do it not for national security, but for profit. The problem is so bad that some experts have coined the term "surveillance capitalism" to describe the practice of collecting user data then selling it for a variety of purposes, all unknown to the people whose data is being traded.

But it's not just companies keen to make a profit on our data. Employers are also increasingly spying on their employees as those workers labor from home. The number of employees who work from home increased dramatically during the COVID-19 pandemic. This led to an increase in their employers tracking them. The practice seems creepy, but employers argue that it is necessary not only to make sure workers remain productive, but to protect company secrets. The authors in this chapter look at both sides of the issue. However, they largely see the practice as a dangerous violation of privacy and detrimental to the relationship between workers and their bosses.

In this chapter, the authors examine the problem, offering some details about who is collecting data on you and what they are doing with it. They also consider the ethical issues surrounding the practice of employers monitoring their employees via computers they use to work from home.

The closing viewpoint asks what those being spied on have to say about it. Not surprisingly, Americans are concerned about the practice, but sadly, feel there is not much they can do about it.

Viewpoint 1

> "Kochava takes location data, aggregates it with other data and links it to consumer identities. The data it sells reveals precise information about a person."

Companies Are Collecting, Analyzing, and Selling Your Data

Anne Toomey McKenna

In this viewpoint, Anne Toomey McKenna examines a lawsuit the Federal Trade Commission (FTC) has filed against the data broker Kochava. The case revolves around Kochava's secretive collection of consumer data, especially location data, which it then uses AI-aided analytics to link to consumer identities. The company then sells this data to its customers, who use this data to target very specific consumers. The FTC asserted that Kochava collected sensitive location data that allows others to identify who goes to places like homeless and domestic abuse shelters, reproductive health clinics, and addiction recovery centers, which could result in stigma, discrimination, or even violence against these people. Anne Toomey McKenna is a visiting professor of law at the University of Richmond.

"Data Brokers Know Everything About You—What FTC Case Against Ad Tech Giant Kochava Reveals," by Anne Toomey McKenna, The Conversation, January 12, 2024, https://theconversation.com/data-brokers-know-everything-about-you-what-ftc-case-against-ad-tech-giant-kochava-reveals-218232. Licensed under CC BY-ND 4.0 International.

As you read, consider the following questions:

1. According to the author, why do data privacy laws not address the role of AI? Is anything being done about this?
2. According to this viewpoint, what is "Kochava Collective" data?
3. What role does AI play in reducing consumer privacy?

Kochava, the self-proclaimed industry leader in mobile app data analytics, is locked in a legal battle with the Federal Trade Commission in a case that could lead to big changes in the global data marketplace and in Congress' approach to artificial intelligence and data privacy.

The stakes are high because Kochava's secretive data acquisition and AI-aided analytics practices are commonplace in the global location data market. In addition to numerous lesser-known data brokers, the mobile data market includes larger players like Foursquare and data market exchanges like Amazon's AWS Data Exchange. The FTC's recently unsealed amended complaint against Kochava makes clear that there's truth to what Kochava advertises: it can provide data for "Any Channel, Any Device, Any Audience," and buyers can "Measure Everything with Kochava."

Separately, the FTC is touting a settlement it just reached with data broker Outlogic, in what it calls the "first-ever ban on the use and sale of sensitive location data." Outlogic has to destroy the location data it has and is barred from collecting or using such information to determine who comes and goes from sensitive locations, like health care centers, homeless and domestic abuse shelters, and religious places.

According to the FTC and proposed class-action lawsuits against Kochava on behalf of adults and children, the company secretly collects, without notice or consent, and otherwise obtains vast amounts of consumer location and personal data. It then analyzes that data using AI, which allows it to predict and influence

Customers Are Skeptical of How Companies Use Their Data

Customers are becoming increasingly wary of the personal data they share with businesses. At the same time, the demand for highly personalized brand interactions has never been greater.

A recent Verizon study found that 45 percent of young customers (ages 18 to 24) would share personal data in exchange for a more intuitive and personalized user experience. Yet 69 percent of all customers who were polled, regardless of age, stated they would avoid companies that have a history of data breaches.

Businesses must be able to balance the collection of customer data with the need for data privacy in order to provide the personalization consumers expect, without compromising or exploiting their information. The key is prioritizing customer transparency—this helps you deliver a superior experience, establish trust, and foster loyalty.

Why Is Customer Transparency Important?

Seventy-five percent of consumers will spend more to buy from a company that treats them well, according to the Zendesk Customer Experience Trends Report 2021. But what does it mean to treat your customers well? Customer satisfaction doesn't hinge solely on perks, gifts, proper pricing, and polite communication. Now more than ever, customer transparency and honesty are essential business practices.

Customers Are Already Skeptical of How Companies Use Their Data

Transparency around how businesses capture, use, and share personal data now plays a critical role in any customer-company relationship, especially given how many consumers don't trust the way businesses are using their personal information.

- In a 2020 McKinsey survey, 71 percent of customers reported that they would leave a company if it shared their sensitive data without permission.
- Even younger generations care immensely about data privacy. According to Internet Innovation Alliance research, nearly three

> out of four Millennials are concerned with how technology and social media companies use their data and location information.
> - A Cisco study revealed that 40 percent of customers don't trust that organizations are following their own data privacy policies.
>
> The good news? Companies can gain customer trust by being more open about their data use policies. A recent Sprout Social survey showed that nearly nine in 10 people would be willing to give second chances after a poor customer experience when an organization is transparent and has a history of transparency. And the 2021 Cisco Data Privacy Benchmark Study found that companies, on average, saw nearly double the returns for every dollar spent on privacy, with wide-ranging benefits:
>
> - 76 percent saw a significant boost in customer trust
> - 73 percent said it made them more attractive
> - 73 percent said it enabled innovation
>
> Prioritizing data transparency as an integral part of your company culture pays off—both for your customers and your business.
>
> [...]
>
> "Customer transparency: Why it matters and how to increase it," by David Galic, *Zendesk Blog*, June 8, 2023.

consumer behavior in an impressively varied and alarmingly invasive number of ways, and serves it up for sale.

Kochava has denied the FTC's allegations.

The FTC says Kochava sells a "360-degree perspective" on individuals and advertises it can "connect precise geolocation data with email, demographics, devices, households, and channels." In other words, Kochava takes location data, aggregates it with other data and links it to consumer identities. The data it sells reveals precise information about a person, such as visits to hospitals, "reproductive health clinics, places of worship, homeless and domestic violence shelters, and addiction recovery facilities." Moreover, by selling such detailed data about people, the FTC says "Kochava is enabling others to identify individuals and exposing them to threats of stigma, stalking, discrimination, job loss, and even physical violence."

I'm a lawyer and law professor practicing, teaching and researching about AI, data privacy and evidence. These complaints underscore for me that U.S. law has not kept pace with regulation of commercially available data or governance of AI.

Most data privacy regulations in the U.S. were conceived in the pre-generative AI era, and there is no overarching federal law that addresses AI-driven data processing. There are Congressional efforts to regulate the use of AI in decision making, like hiring and sentencing. There are also efforts to provide public transparency around AI's use. But Congress has yet to pass legislation.

What Litigation Documents Reveal

According to the FTC, Kochava secretly collects and then sells its "Kochava Collective" data, which includes precise geolocation data, comprehensive profiles of individual consumers, consumers' mobile app use details and Kochava's "audience segments."

The FTC says Kochava's audience segments can be based on "behaviors" and sensitive information such as gender identity, political and religious affiliation, race, visits to hospitals and abortion clinics, and people's medical information, like menstruation and ovulation, and even cancer treatments. By selecting certain audience segments, Kochava customers can identify and target extremely specific groups. For example, this could include people who gender identify as "other," or all the pregnant females who are African American and Muslim. The FTC says selected audience segments can be narrowed to a specific geographical area or, conceivably, even down to a specific building.

By identify, the FTC explains that Kochava customers are able to obtain the name, home address, email address, economic status and stability, and much more data about people within selected groups. This data is purchased by organizations like advertisers, insurers and political campaigns that seek to narrowly classify and target people. The FTC also says it can be purchased by people who want to harm others.

How Kochava Acquires Such Sensitive Data

The FTC says Kochava acquires consumer data in two ways: through Kochava's software development kits that it provides to app developers, and directly from other data brokers. The FTC says those Kochava-supplied software development kits are installed in over 10,000 apps globally. Kochava's kits, embedded with Kochava's coding, collect hordes of data and send it back to Kochava without the consumer being told or consenting to the data collection.

Another lawsuit against Kochava in California alleges similar charges of surreptitious data collection and analysis, and that Kochava sells customized data feeds based on extremely sensitive and private information precisely tailored to its clients' needs.

AI Pierces Your Privacy

The FTC's complaint also illustrates how advancing AI tools are enabling a new phase in data analysis. Generative AI's ability to process vast amounts of data is reshaping what can be done with and learned from mobile data in ways that invade privacy. This includes inferring and disclosing sensitive or otherwise legally protected information, like medical records and images.

AI provides the ability both to know and predict just about anything about individuals and groups, even very sensitive behavior. It also makes it possible to manipulate individual and group behavior, inducing decisions in favor of the specific users of the AI tool.

This type of "AI coordinated manipulation" can supplant your decision-making ability without your knowledge.

Privacy in the Balance

The FTC enforces laws against unfair and deceptive business practices, and it informed Kochava in 2022 that the company was in violation. Both sides have had some wins and losses in the ongoing case. Senior U.S. District Judge B. Lynn Winmill, who is overseeing the case, dismissed the FTC's first complaint and required more facts from the FTC. The commission filed an amended complaint that provided much more specific allegations.

Winmill has not yet ruled on another Kochava motion to dismiss the FTC's case, but as of a Jan. 3, 2024 filing in the case, the parties are proceeding with discovery. A 2025 trial date is expected, but the date has not yet been set.

For now, companies, privacy advocates and policymakers are likely keeping an eye on this case. Its outcome, combined with proposed legislation and the FTC's focus on generative AI, data and privacy, could spell big changes for how companies acquire data, the ways that AI tools can be used to analyze data, and what data can lawfully be used in machine- and human-based data analytics.

VIEWPOINT 2

> "Companies need to adopt an 'ethics of care' approach to their workers, meaning they make a commitment to take care of them. They need to investigate their surveillance practices and analyse how exactly line managers use them to check up on workers."

Employee Surveillance Lowers Worker Morale and Should Be Curbed

Evronia Azer

In this viewpoint, Evronia Azer explains how the rise of remote working since the start of the COVID-19 pandemic has prompted more employers to use digital surveillance on their employees. This is often justified in the name of productivity, since employers are concerned their employees are putting in less effort since they work from home. However, Azer asserts that surveillance has a negative impact on workplaces by causing employees to feel afraid and distrustful of their employers and reducing their job satisfaction and morale. She argues that employers and regulators should attempt to address the emotional and privacy impacts of this type of surveillance. Evronia Azer is an assistant professor at the Centre for Business in Society at Coventry University.

"Remote Working Has Led to Managers Spying on Staff—Here Are Three Ways to Curb It," by Evronia Azer, The Conversation, May 6, 2021, https://theconversation.com/remote-working-has-led-to-managers-spying-more-on-staff-here-are-three-ways-to-curb-it-159604. Licensed under CC BY-ND 4.0 International.

Espionage and Intelligence

As you read, consider the following questions:

1. According to this viewpoint, how do managers keep track of their employees' productivity?
2. What factors does this viewpoint mention could potentially cause an employee to be more sensitive to workplace surveillance?
3. How does Azer think that the focus of research on workplace surveillance should change?

With so many more people working from home during the pandemic, employers have stepped up the extent to which they are monitoring them online. Not so many years ago, employees were having to adjust to having their work emails monitored; but that seems almost quaint compared to the digital surveillance we are seeing today.

Employers can use specialist software to track workers' keystrokes, mouse movements and the websites they visit. They can take screenshots of employees to check whether they are at their screens and looking attentive, or even use webcam monitoring software that measures things like eye movements, facial expressions and body language. All this can be checked against a worker's output to draw conclusions about their productivity.

Besides specialist software, managers can view statistics from their corporate private network to see who logged in and for what duration, and again cross-reference this to workers' productivity data. In some organisations, staff who do not open work applications early in the morning could potentially be viewed as late for work or not productive enough.

Home-working has also raised the prospect of more informal staff monitoring. For example, if a worker would normally log in to meetings by turning on their video, but one day they are in a car or a new location, the employer might think they are not committed or focused enough.

This all raises questions about how such surveillance is affecting people's work practices, privacy and general wellbeing. Given that home-working looks set to extend beyond lockdown for many people, this is clearly a moment for some serious reflection.

The Productivity Dimension

Managers justify this kind of surveillance by claiming that it is good for productivity. Some workers even seem to agree with this – provided the monitoring is done by a peer and not a manager.

Many have signed up to an online service called Focusmate, for example, which matches anonymous strangers on "work dates" where they briefly say what they will be doing during the appointment and then they can rate one another's approach to work at the end. The service aims to make workers more productive and to feel less lonely at work.

That said, home-working during the first UK lockdown in spring 2020 did not have a major effect on productivity. Workplace surveillance may even have held it back, given that it appears to have increased at the same time. Certainly, there is evidence thatsuch techniques can make people feel vulnerable, afraid and less creative. It can also reduce their job satisfaction and lower their morale.

Next Steps

In view of all this, companies need to adopt an "ethics of care" approach to their workers, meaning they make a commitment to take care of them. They need to investigate their surveillance practices and analyse how exactly line managers use them to check up on workers.

While carrying out such an investigation, companies should recognise that some employees might be finding workplace surveillance more difficult than others. This will depend on to what extent they think it invades their privacy, and how they weigh the risks and benefits of sharing their data.

This is likely to be affected by things like their cultural background, gender and the context in question. Those already struggling with home-working, perhaps because they have to care for children at the same time, are particularly likely to feel that this surveillance is making their lives even harder. Workers can therefore try and evade surveillance techniques – for example, by keeping an automatic mouse-moving application open to make sure they appear online all the time.

Companies should be ensuring from these investigations that employees are aware of what data is collected about them and how it's used. They should hold open discussions with workers and unions on how these monitoring practices affect workers, and allow workers to have their say without threatening disciplinary action. If workers feel that their employers care about them as individuals, they will hopefully feel empowered and trusting towards them, and less likely to find workarounds or to react negatively.

Equally, it is important for regulators like the UK Information Commissioner to reflect on how surveillance in the workplace is changing. The UK code in this area broadly requires that any monitoring be fair to workers and that any adverse impacts – for example, on workers' privacy, damage to trust, or demeaning workers – be mitigated. The rules may now need to be updated to reflect some of the latest forms of surveillance, and there is a role for researchers in looking into this as well.

Researchers have tended to look at workplace surveillance from the perspective of productivity where workers are viewed as resources, but we need to start thinking in terms of data justice. This has been described as "fairness in the way people are made visible, represented and treated as a result of their production of digital data."

In a world where computers and smartphones are all around us, we need to negotiate our private spaces and our control over the data we produce online. Just like this has implications in our private lives for our relationship with Facebook or Google, the increases in workplace surveillance make it just as important at work.

VIEWPOINT 3

> "These devices are indiscriminate. If you're working from home they can pick up audio and visual images of your private life."

Privacy Law Isn't Keeping Up with Technology

Jacqueline Meredith and Peter Holland

The previous viewpoint discussed monitoring of employees by their employers. Here, the authors explore the question of whether your employer is required to tell you if they are spying on you by examining the Australian legal framework. The authors suggest that the law struggles to keep up with advancements in surveillance technology. Jacqueline Meredith is a lecturer at Swinburne Law School in Australia and a member of the Centre for Employment and Labour Relations Law at Melbourne Law School. Peter Holland is a professor in human resource management and employee relations at the Swinburne Business School.

As you read, consider the following questions:

1. What, according to these authors, is "productivity paranoia," and how can that hurt workers?
2. What aspects of this kind of tracking are legitimate, according to Meredith and Holland?

"Does your employer have to tell if they're spying on you through your work computer?," by Jacqueline Meredith and Peter Holland, The Conversation, October 9, 2023. https://theconversation.com/does-your-employer-have-to-tell-if-theyre-spying-on-you-through-your-work-computer-214857. Licensed under CC BY-ND 4.0 International.

3. What advice do the authors offer employees who think they're being monitored?

The COVID pandemic stimulated an irreversible shift in where, when and how we work. This 21st-century model of working – dubbed the "new normal" – is characterised by increased flexibility and productivity gains.

Yet this reshaping of work, underpinned by technology, has also eroded our work-life boundaries – and persisting 20th-century attitudes are preventing us from successfully managing the new normal.

We find ourselves struggling with "productivity paranoia": a term used to describe managers' concerns that remote and hybrid workers aren't doing enough when not under supervision.

As a result, we're seeing a surge in the use of electronic monitoring and surveillance devices in the workplace. These devices allow managers to "watch over" employees in their absence. This practice raises serious legal and ethical concerns.

Big Bossware Is Here

In a survey of 20,000 people across 11 countries, Microsoft reported 85% of managers struggled to trust their remote-working employees. In Australia, this figure was 90%.

In 2021, American research and consulting firm Gartner estimated the number of large firms tracking, monitoring and surveilling their workers had doubled to 60% since the start of the pandemic.

Electronic monitoring and surveillance technology can capture screenshots of an employee's computer, record their keystrokes and mouse movements, and even activate their webcam or microphones.

On one hand, these "bossware" tools can be used to capture employee and production statistics, providing businesses with useful evidence-based analytics.

The other side is much darker. These devices are indiscriminate. If you're working from home they can pick up audio and visual images of your private life.

Managers can be sent notifications when data "indicate" an employee is taking breaks or getting distracted.

Some aspects of electronic monitoring and surveillance are legitimate. For instance, it may be necessary to safeguard an organisation's data access and transfers.

But where are the boundaries? Is your organisation legally obliged to tell you about electronic intrusions? Alternatively, what can you do if you find out you're being watched without being informed?

The Legal Framework

A complex array of regulation governs workplace privacy and surveillance in Australia. Proposed reforms to the Privacy Act 1988 are set to strengthen privacy protections for private-sector employees.

However, this legislation doesn't specifically cover workplace surveillance. Instead, a patchwork of laws in each state and territory regulate this matter.

Specific legislation regulates the surveillance of workers in New South Wales and the Australian Capital Territory. Importantly, surveillance must not be undertaken unless the employer has provided at least 14 days' notice. This notice must include specific details about the surveillance that will be carried out. Employers must also develop and adhere to a surveillance policy.

In both states, employers can only record visual images of an employee while they're "at work". This is broadly defined to capture any place where work is carried out.

Covert surveillance is prohibited unless the employer has obtained a court order. In this case it's restricted to situations where the employee is suspected of unlawful activity.

Even then, a covert surveillance order would not be granted where this unduly intrudes on the employee's privacy. Covert surveillance for the purpose of monitoring work performance is expressly prohibited.

Other states and territories don't have specific electronic workplace surveillance laws. Employers must instead comply with more general surveillance legislation.

Broadly speaking, employees must give consent, express or implied, to any surveillance. In practice, such consent is usually obtained through the implementation of a workplace surveillance policy, which employees must agree to when they accept the job. So if you've signed a contract without reading the fine print, you may have agreed to being surveilled via electronic monitoring tools.

Currently, Queensland and Tasmania provide the most limited protection for employees. Their surveillance legislation is limited to the regulation of listening devices.

Enterprise agreements, employment contracts and workplace policies may also limit or prohibit the use of surveillance devices. In practice, however, most employees will lack the bargaining power to negotiate the inclusion of any such terms in their employment contract.

The Law Is Failing to Keep Up

In 2022, a parliamentary select committee reporting on the future of work in NSW observed the current regulatory framework is failing to keep pace with rapid advancements in electronic monitoring and surveillance.

The report criticised legislation that simply allows an employer to notify workers surveillance will be carried out, with no mechanism for this to be negotiated or challenged. The situation is slightly better in the ACT, where employers must consult with workers in good faith about any proposed surveillance activities.

Workers who suspect their employer is spying on them should review their workplace surveillance policies. They may need to reflect carefully on how they use their work computer.

Where an enterprise agreement applies, the Fair Work Commission can arbitrate surveillance disputes. A worker who is dismissed following intrusive surveillance may be able to challenge the dismissal on the basis of it being unfair.

Workers who haven't been informed of their employer's surveillance practices can also lodge a complaint with the relevant authority or regulator, who may have powers to investigate and prosecute offences.

To thrive in our "new normal" work landscape, we'll need to address the gap between the existing legal protections and the capabilities (and potential harms) of electronic monitoring and surveillance. For now, it remains a significant legal and ethical challenge.

VIEWPOINT 4

> "In January 2021, reports emerged that one in five companies were using surveillance software to remotely monitor their employees—in some cases without the employees' knowledge or consent."

Watching Workers Is Ethically Questionable and Not Always Productive

Linda Rodriguez McRobbie

In this viewpoint, Linda Rodriguez McRobbie discusses the effects of monitoring workers, not on their productivity but on their behavior, for better or for worse. She also addresses the question of whether or not it is ethically right to surveil workers—or even if it is productive. The traditional logic has been that measuring productivity helps keep workers accountable, but evidence suggests that it actually undermines trust between employees and employers. Linda Rodriguez McRobbie is an American journalist and author living in England.

As you read, consider the following questions:

1. How, according to studies cited in this viewpoint, does being watched affect behavior?

"Is it right or productive to watch workers?," by Linda Rodriguez McRobbie, *Strategy+Business*, October 18, 2021. Reprinted by permission.

2. According to data cited in this viewpoint, how did the increase in remote working that occurred during the pandemic impact productivity?
3. According to this viewpoint, does watching workers improve their productivity?

It goes without saying that the biggest shift in the workplace over the last two years has been its disappearance. Or rather, its retreat from the physical world and its reemergence in the work-anywhere digital limbo of Zoom meetings and Slack channels. And, with a few caveats, the robust conclusion has been that, yes, remote employees can still get their work done from their kitchen table, their spare bedroom, their shed, or the patio of their favorite coffee shop.

But let's be honest: the office isn't merely a place to do work—it can also be the place to be *observed* doing work. Which is why a significant number of companies whose workforce has recently gone remote have enlisted the help of surveillance software, also known as "tattleware" or "bossware," to know what their employees are doing.

There's an old saw in business: what gets measured gets managed. That has been elevated to gospel when it comes to raw materials, waste, energy use, emissions, and so forth. Viewed this way, surveillance tech may not be an altogether bad idea. There is value in measuring what your employees are doing and how productive they are. What makes surveillance challenging is connecting it to management, or even control.

In January 2021, reports emerged that one in five companies were using surveillance software to remotely monitor their employees—in some cases without the employees' knowledge or consent. Where monitoring software had once been a relatively small market, populated by benign-sounding products like Hubstaff, ActivTrak, Workpuls, and Time Doctor, it's grown. A lot.

Concrete numbers are difficult to come by, but, according to analysis from Top10VPN released in August, US demand for employee surveillance software is up 58% since 2020. The same report noted that in April 2020, as the full implications of lockdowns and work-from-home orders were realized, demand for employee monitoring software soared 87% and fell only slightly, to 71% above the pre-pandemic average, a month later.

Since then, employee monitoring software has remained a booming business. And for people who like privacy and employers who want to have a good relationship with their employees, that may not be a good thing.

"When the pandemic hits, you suddenly see the reality, which is that [organizations] don't trust employees, they never did," Ben Laker, professor of leadership at Henley Business School, near London, told me. "Suddenly organizations are panicking—*how can we control [our workers] if we can't see them?* At that very core, there's just no trust."

Surveillance tech can include taking screenshots of an employee's computer at regular intervals, tracking what websites they visit during company hours, monitoring their keystrokes and mouse movement, and even noting their remote location, allowing employers to know whether their workers are at their desks in their home offices, getting lunch, or picking up their children from school. The ostensible purpose of monitoring is often "increased productivity." But the big question is: is it worth it?

Positive Reinforcement?

Studies demonstrate that being watched reinforces positive socially normative behaviors and inhibits negative behaviors. If you think you're being observed, for example, you're more likely to donate to charity and less likely to litter, steal a bike, or take too much Halloween candy. And there are, theoretically, valid positive reasons for monitoring, including to safeguard employees from internal discrimination and harassment; employees can also use the collected data to, as one academic put it, "stare back" at employers and expose problematic or even dangerous practices through whistleblowing.

But even back in the 1980s, with the minimal electronic surveillance available, employees whose performance was monitored perceived their working conditions as more stressful and reported higher levels of job boredom, fatigue, anger, anxiety, and even depression and other health complaints. Observers, including in places like the *Wall Street Journal*, worried that electronic surveillance would turn the modern office into "fishbowls" and "sweatshops."

Workplace surveillance, however, continued, despite evidence that it tended to undermine trust between employee and employer. And now, the shift to remote working has meant that surveillance that was once limited to the office is happening, well, anywhere the employee is. Almost nowhere is safe from Big Brother.

In some cases, though, there is evidence that monitoring doesn't promote productivity or curb negative behaviors. For one thing, remote workers are already more productive, monitoring or no. An April 2021 Bloomberg report found that working from home during the pandemic lifted productivity 5% across the US. What's more, monitoring can backfire. In a 2011 study, computer monitoring that employees felt violated their privacy increased employees' destructive behavior. Henley Business School's Laker suggests that employees who are over-monitored are robbed of a sense of freedom and autonomy, which can in turn undercut their performance. "Without autonomy, [employees] won't master [new skills] and they won't have purpose," he told me.

Privacy Matters

Any discussion of surveillance, however, must take into account the world we inhabit now. The concerns that we had about physical and digital privacy even five years ago are not the same ones we have currently. Conversations about what it means to be private are shaped by the convenience and ubiquity of social media, big data, and what Australian Roger Clarke, a consultant and research professor, described in 2019 as the "digital surveillance economy."

The recent rise in employee surveillance accelerated during the pandemic, largely because it had to, but the bottom line is that we are now more than ever accustomed to being watched. We accept the intrusion of cameras in novel spaces under the promise of increased safety; doorbell cameras spring to mind, but so too do webcams and smartphones; we accept data tracking to prove we're "not a robot" on websites; we accept that our information, our clicks, and our preferences are observed and noted.

We seem to be primed now to accept that companies have a reasonable expectation to protect their own safety, so to speak, by monitoring *us*. One recent survey by media researcher Clutch of 400 US workers found that only 22% of 18- to 34-year-old employees were concerned about their employers having access to their personal information and activity from their work computers. Meanwhile, in a pre-pandemic survey of US workers by US media group Axios from August 2019, 62% of respondents agreed that employers should be able to use technology to monitor employees.

And yet, despite the possibility that increased acceptance might mitigate some of monitoring's negative impacts, it's hard to get past the inherently icky nature of surveillance. "Show me someone who wants to be surveilled," Laker said.

So, is there a way to ethically, appropriately monitor workers? A lot of that comes down to how the employees themselves feel about being monitored. Amy Vatcha of the London School of Economics wrote in a 2020 paper that employee acceptance of workplace monitoring "depends on these factors—transparency on data collection from employers, clarification of data usage for system security or for hiring and firing decisions, and the avenues available for employee privacy concerns to be heard."

Espionage and Intelligence

    These sound like sensible measures, but it's hard to imagine that all the companies that have rushed to install the technology have thought through these protocols. So maybe the solution to maintaining increased productivity and keeping the remote office bumping along is to *trust* employees and leave the spyware alone.

VIEWPOINT 5

> "About six-in-ten Americans believe it is not possible to go through daily life without having their data collected by companies"

Most Americans Are Concerned About the Use of Their Data

Brooke Auxier and Lee Rainie

In this viewpoint, which is a summary of a national survey that was conducted by the Pew Research Center, Americans have their say about privacy, surveillance, and the sale of their data. Most are not pleased. Many feel that their privacy is being violated and that their data is less secure than it has been in the past. The problem is made worse by the fact that most Americans have little understanding of the data privacy laws that exist. Brooke Auxier is a technology researcher and former research associate at Pew Research Center. Lee Rainie is former director of internet and technology research at Pew.

As you read, consider the following questions:

1. According to this survey, what percentage of Americans think their online activities are being tracked by companies?

"Key takeaways on Americans' views about privacy, surveillance and data-sharing," by Brooke Auxier and Lee Rainie, Pew Research Center, November 15, 2019.

2. According to the data cited in this viewpoint, do most Americans feel like they understand what is being done with their data?
3. What do most Americans think should be done in response to excessive data collection?

In key ways, today's digitally networked society runs on quid pro quos: People exchange details about themselves and their activities for services and products on the web or apps. Many are willing to accept the deals they are offered in return for sharing insight about their purchases, behaviors and social lives. At times, their personal information is collected by government on the grounds that there are benefits to public safety and security.

A majority of Americans are concerned about this collection and use of their data, according to a new report from Pew Research Center.

Here are 10 key takeaways from the report:

Americans Are Concerned About How Much Data Is Being Collected About Them, and Many Feel Their Information Is Less Secure than It Used to Be

The majority of Americans say they are at least somewhat concerned about how much data is collected about them by both companies (79%) and the government (64%). Additionally, seven-in-ten Americans say they feel their personal information is less secure than it was five years ago. This compares with just 6% who say they feel their information is more secure, and about one-quarter (24%) who feel it's about the same.

A Majority of the Public Believes Much of Their Online Activities Are Being Tracked

More Americans say they think that what they do online or on their cellphone is being tracked than believe their *offline* activities are tracked. They are also more likely to believe companies track more of their activities (both online and off) than think that the government is collecting information on them. For example, the majority of Americans believe that all or most of what they do online and on their cellphone is being tracked by companies (72%), while just 47% think the same of the government. Smaller shares believe all or most of their offline activities (like where they go and who they talk to) are being tracked by companies (31%) and the government (24%).

Large Shares of Americans Do Not Think It Is Possible to Go About Daily Life Without Corporate and Government Entities Collecting Data About Them

About six-in-ten Americans believe it is not possible to go through daily life without having their data collected by companies (62%) or the government (63%). However, 38% of U.S. adults do believe it is possible to go untracked by companies in daily life, and 36% say the same about the government.

A Majority of U.S. Adults Have Heard at Least a Little About How Companies and Other Organizations Use Their Data to Target Them with Ads

One way that companies and other organizations use data – like people's purchasing and credit histories, and their online browsing and search behaviors – is to build out user data profiles in order to serve them targeted ads, offer special deals or assess how risky people might be as customers. Some 77% of U.S. adults have heard at least a little bit about this concept, and, of those who have, 75% say they think all or most companies use this tactic to help understand their customers.

Very Few Americans Believe They Understand What Is Being Done with the Data Collected About Them

Small shares of Americans say they understand a great deal about what is being done with the data collected about them by companies (6%) or the government (4%). By contrast, around eight-in-ten Americans (78%) say they understand very little or nothing about what the government does with the personal data it collects, compared with a smaller share – though still a majority – who say the same about company-collected data (59%).

Almost All Americans Have Been Asked to Agree to Privacy Policies, but Fewer Actually Read Them

Some 97% of U.S. adults have ever been asked to agree to company privacy policy, which includes 25% who say they are asked to do this almost daily. Yet only about 20% of Americans overall say they always (9%) or often (13%) read these policies before agreeing to them, and 36% say they never read them. Among those who say they ever read such policies, about one-in-five (22%) say they read privacy policies all the way through and that they are more likely to say they glance over these policies without reading them closely.

Most Americans See More Risks than Benefits from Personal Data Collection

About eight-in-ten (81%) Americans say the potential risks outweigh the benefits when it comes to companies collecting data. When government collection of data is considered, 66% of adults agree. Americans don't feel they benefit personally from the data collection, either. Just 5% of adults say they benefit a great deal from the data companies collect about them, and 4% say the same about government's data collection.

Americans Vary in Their Attitudes Toward Data-Sharing in Pursuit of Public Good

Though many Americans don't think they benefit much from the collection of their data, and they find that the potential risks of this practice outweigh the benefits, there are some scenarios in which the public is more likely to accept the idea of data-sharing. In line with findings in a 2015 Center survey showing that some Americans are comfortable with trade-offs in sharing data, about half of U.S. adults (49%) say it is acceptable for the government to collect data about all Americans in order to assess potential terrorist threats. That compares with 31% who feel it is unacceptable to collect data about all Americans for that purpose. By contrast, just one-quarter say it is acceptable for smart speaker makers to share users' audio recordings with law enforcement to help with criminal investigations, versus 49% who find that unacceptable.

The Majority of the Public Does Not Feel in Control of the Data Collected About Them

More than eight-in-ten (84%) of Americans say they feel very little or no control over the data collected about them by the government, and 81% say the same when company data collection is considered. Just 4% of U.S. adults say they have a great deal of control over data collected by the government, and 3% agree regarding companies' collection of information.

Americans Say They Have Very Little Understanding of Current Data Protection Laws, and Most Are in Favor of More Government Regulation

Just 3% of U.S. adults say they have "a lot" of understanding of the current laws and regulations in place to protect their data privacy, with 63% saying they understand very little or not at all. A majority of Americans say they have little or no understanding of existing data protection laws. However, the majority of Americans support more government regulation in this area. Some 75% of U.S. adults say there should be more government regulation of what companies can do with customers' personal information. These numbers echo figures from an earlier Pew Research Center phone survey from 2013, not based on the American Trends Panel, which found that 68% of internet users believed the current laws weren't good enough at protecting people's privacy online.

These findings come from a survey of 4,272 U.S. adults conducted on Pew Research Center's American Trends Panel between June 3 and 17, 2019. It has an overall margin of error of plus or minus 1.87 percentage points.

Periodical and Internet Sources Bibliography

The following articles have been selected to supplement the diverse views presented in this chapter

Bobby Allyn, "Your Boss Is Watching You: Work-From-Home Boom Leads to More Surveillance," NPR, May 13, 2020. https://www.npr.org/2020/05/13/854014403/your-boss-is-watching-you-work-from-home-boom-leads-to-more-surveillance.

Lois Beckett, "Yes, Companies Are Harvesting – and Selling – Your Facebook Profile," ProPublica, November 9, 2012. https://www.propublica.org/article/yes-companies-are-harvesting-and-selling-your-social-media-profiles.

Pia Ceres, "Kids Are Back in Classrooms and Laptops Are Still Spying on Them," *Wired*, August 3, 2022. https://www.wired.com/story/student-monitoring-software-privacy-in-schools/.

Alexander Furnas, "Everything You Wanted to Know About Data Mining but Were Afraid to Ask," the *Atlantic*, April 3, 2012. https://www.theatlantic.com/technology/archive/2012/04/everything-you-wanted-to-know-about-data-mining-but-were-afraid-to-ask/255388/.

Saul Gravy, "High Tech Is Watching You," *Harvard Gazette*, March 4, 2019. https://news.harvard.edu/gazette/story/2019/03/harvard-professor-says-surveillance-capitalism-is-undermining-democracy/.

Eric Johnson, "Google and Facebook Have Become 'Antithetical to Democracy,' says *The Age of Surveillance Capitalism* Author Shoshana Zuboff," *Vox*, February 20, 2019. https://www.vox.com/2019/2/20/18232469/shoshana-zuboff-age-surveillance-capitalism-book-google-facebook-privacy-data-kara-swisher.

Will Knight, "Generative AI Is Making Companies Even More Thirsty for Your Data," *Wired*, August 18, 2023. https://www.wired.com/story/fast-forward-generative-ai-companies-thirsty-for-your-data/.

Nir Kshetri, "School Surveillance of Students via Laptops May Do More Harm Than Good," the *Conversation*, November 9, 2021.

https://theconversation.com/school-surveillance-of-students-via-laptops-may-do-more-harm-than-good-170983.

Alexis C. Madrigal, "Facebook Didn't Sell Your Data; It Gave It Away (In exchange for even more data about you from Amazon, Netflix, Spotify, Microsoft, and others)" the *Atlantic*, December 19, 2018. https://www.theatlantic.com/technology/archive/2018/12/facebooks-failures-and-also-its-problems-leaking-data/578599/.

Heidi N. Moore, "Why Didn't Equifax Protect Your Data? Because Corporations Have All the Power." *Washington Post*, September 21, 2017. https://www.washingtonpost.com/news/posteverything/wp/2017/09/21/why-didnt-equifax-protect-your-data-because-corporations-have-all-the-power/.

Alfred Ng, "What Does It Actually Mean When a Company Says, 'We Do Not Sell Your Data'?" the *Markup*, September 2, 2021. https://themarkup.org/the-breakdown/2021/09/02/what-does-it-actually-mean-when-a-company-says-we-do-not-sell-your-data.

Zeynep Tufekci, "Think You're Discreet Online? Think Again," *New York Times*, April 21, 2019. https://www.nytimes.com/2019/04/21/opinion/computational-inference.html.

Shoshana Zuboff, "You Are Now Remotely Controlled: Surveillance Capitalists Control the Science and the Scientists, the Secrets and the Truth," *New York Times*, January 24, 2020. https://www.nytimes.com/2020/01/24/opinion/sunday/surveillance-capitalism.html.

For Further Discussion

Chapter 1

1. The first viewpoint in this chapter discussed how some of the spies who shared nuclear secrets with the Soviet Union did it for what seemed like a good reason at the time: to ensure nuclear parity between the two nations and thus prevent a nuclear war that could destroy the world. What do you think of this reasoning? Do you think the fact that the U.S. and the U.S.S.R. could easily have destroyed each other did indeed help prevent nuclear war in the years following World War II?
2. Why was the CIA able to get away with a program like MK-ULTRA? Do you think it would have happened if there had been more oversight of the intelligence community? Do you think something like that could happen now? Explain your reasoning.
3. In one viewpoint in this chapter, Marvin C. Ott argues that the state of the relationship between the intelligence community and Congress, the White House, and the public is in such bad shape that it needs to be totally rethought. Why do you think it's difficult for an open society, such as the U.S., to maintain an effective intelligence community? Based on Ott's arguments, what changes would you suggest?

Chapter 2

1. Revelations that U.S. spy agencies had tapped the phones of European leaders temporarily roiled relations between the U.S. and its allies. Germany, in particular, responded harshly. Based on the viewpoints you've read in this chapter, do you think spying on allies is a significant issue? Do you think that the dangers posed by terrorism and other threats justify some level of spying on citizens and allies? Why or why not?

Espionage and Intelligence

2. The viewpoint in this chapter by Eugene Matos and Adrian Zienkiewicz explores the line between diplomacy and espionage. Embassies, it seems, are teeming with spies. However, that is often overlooked by the host nations. Why might this be the case? What is the advantage to a nation of turning a blind eye to spies in embassies?
3. Based on the viewpoints in this chapter, what are the benefits to the countries involved in the Five Eyes alliance? Are there any risks?

Chapter 3

1. Even today, some people think Edward Snowden is a traitor, while others hail him as a hero, or at least a brave whistleblower. Based on what you've read in this chapter, what is your perspective on Snowden's actions? Did the ruling that the NSA's collection program was unconstitutional justify his actions? Why or why not?
2. One of Zachary Keck's arguments in his viewpoint about Edward Snowden is that Snowden fled first to China and then Russia, both adversaries of the United States. Keck seems to believe that Snowden offered U.S. secrets to these nations, perhaps in exchange for protection. Yet had he fled to U.S. allies, they most certainly would have turned him in to the U.S. Do you think the evidence supports Keck's arguments? Can you make a similar claim (no matter what you think of Snowden's guilt or innocence) based on different reasoning?
3. Section 702 of the U.S. Foreign Intelligence Surveillance Act (FISA) is typically reauthorized, but usually after a lot of debate about reforms. And perhaps unusually these days, the debate doesn't split along party lines. Why do you think it is so difficult for Congress to make the reforms needed to protect U.S. citizens from warrantless surveillance?

Chapter 4

1. According to the viewpoints by Anne Toomey McKenna and Brooke Auxier and Lee Rainie, people are clearly unhappy that companies are collecting and selling information about them. Yet, people still use products, such as Facebook, that trade in their data. What do you think persuades people to knowingly allow big companies to invade their privacy and profit from doing so?
2. Based on what you've read in the viewpoints in this chapter, do you think regulation and legislation on data collection can keep up with new technologies? Why or why not?
3. Do you think it is ethical for companies to use surveillance on their employees? Can you think of any situations in which that kind of spying might be justified? Explain your reasoning.

Organizations to Contact

The editors have compiled the following list of organizations concerned with the issues debated in this book. The descriptions are derived from materials provided by the organizations. All have publications or information available for interested readers. The list was compiled on the date of publication of the present volume; the information provided here may change. Be aware that many organizations take several weeks or longer to respond to inquiries, so allow as much time as possible.

American Civil Liberties Union (ACLU)
125 Broad Street, 18th Floor
New York NY 10004
(212) 549-2500
website: www.aclu.org

The ACLU is an organization that has been working since its founding in 1920 to defend and protect the individual rights and liberties that are guaranteed by the Constitution of the United States. One of the issues the organization champions is digital rights and privacy.

Center for a New American Security (CNAS)
1152 15th Street NW
Suite 950
Washington, DC 20005
(202) 457-9400
email: info@cnas.org
website: www.cnas.org

A nonprofit research organization, the CNAS is dedicated to developing strong, pragmatic, and principled national security and defense policies. It provides policymakers with research and analysis on national security and foreign policy.

Center for Strategic and International Studies (CSIS)

1616 Rhode Island Avenue NW
Washington, DC 20036
(202) 887-0200
email: aschwartz@csis.org
website: www.csis.org

The CSIS is a bipartisan nonprofit policy research organization dedicated to advancing practical ideas to address the world's greatest challenges. It works to shape the future of national security through policy expertise, analysis, and research.

Central Intelligence Agency of the United States (CIA)

Office of Public Affairs
Washington, DC 20505
website: www.cia.gov

The CIA is a U.S. government agency that provides intelligence on foreign countries and global issues to the president, the National Security Council, and other policymakers to help them make national security decisions. In addition to collecting and analyzing intelligence, the agency also conducts covert actions as directed by the president.

Electronic Frontier Foundation (EFF)

815 Eddy Street
San Francisco, CA 94109
(415) 436-9333
email: info@eff.org
website: www.eff.org

The Electronic Frontier Foundation is a nonprofit organization working to defend civil liberties in the digital world. One of the key issues the organization supports is protecting digital privacy.

Federal Bureau of Investigation (FBI)

935 Pennsylvania Avenue NW
Washington, DC 20535
(202) 324-3000
website: www.fbi.gov

The FBI is the principal federal law enforcement agency and domestic intelligence and security service of the United States. Some of the bureau's objectives are to expose, prevent, and investigate intelligence activities within the U.S. and to protect the U.S. intelligence community.

George Washington's Mount Vernon

3200 Mount Vernon Memorial Highway
Mount Vernon, VA 22121
(703) 780-2000
email: tickets@mountvernon.org
website: www.mountvernon.org/george-washington/the-revolutionary-war/spying-and-espionage/

George Washington's home, Mount Vernon, is maintained by the Mount Vernon Ladies Association and has educational exhibits about spying and espionage during the Revolutionary War. You can find information about Revolutionary War espionage on its website.

Intelligence and National Security Alliance (INSA)

(703) 224-4672
email: info@insaonline,org
website: www.insaonline.org

A nonprofit organization dedicated to addressing contemporary intelligence and national security challenges, INSA facilitates public discourse on the role and value of intelligence for the nation's security. It also advances the intelligence field as a career choice by offering scholarships to graduate and undergraduate students.

International Spy Museum

700 L'Enfant Plaza SW
Washington DC 20024
(202) 393-7798
email: info@spymuseum.org
website: www.spymuseum.org

The International Spy Museum is home to the world's largest collection of espionage artifacts on display. This includes exhibits that highlight the changing role of technology in intelligence work.

National Security Agency (NSA)

9800 Savage Road, Suite 6272
Fort George G. Meade, MD 20755
(301) 688-6311
website: www.nsa.gov

The NSA is the U.S. intelligence agency responsible for the global monitoring, collection, and processing of information and data for foreign and domestic intelligence and counterintelligence purposes. It aids in cybersecurity efforts and provides foreign signals intelligence (SIGINT) to the country's policymakers and military.

Bibliography of Books

Kai Bird. *American Prometheus: The Triumph and Tragedy of J. Robert Oppenheimer.* New York, NY: Knopf, 2005.

Cory Doctorow. *How to Destroy Surveillance Capitalism.* New York, NY: Stonesong Digital, 2020.

Amaryllis Fox. *Life Undercover: Coming of Age in the CIA.* New York, NY: Vintage, 2019.

Michael Holzman. *Spies and Traitors: Kim Philby, James Angleton and the Friendship and Betrayal that Would Shape MI6, the CIA and the Cold War.* New York, NY: Pegasus, 2021.

Avery Elizabeth Hurt. *Codebreakers and Spies of the Cold War.* New York, NY: Cavendish Square, 2018.

Jack Kelly. *God Save Benedict Arnold: The True Story of America's Most Hated Man.* New York, NY: St. Martin's, 2023.

Dave Lindorff. *Spy for No Country: The Story of Ted Hall, the Teenage Atomic Spy Who May Have Saved the World.* Lanham, MD: Prometheus, 2024.

Ben Macintyre. *The Spy and the Traitor: The Greatest Espionage Story of the Cold War.* New York, NY: Crown, 2019.

Liza Mundy. *Code Girls: The Untold Story of the American Women Code Breakers of World War II.* New York, NY: Hachette, 2017.

David H. Price. *The American Surveillance State: How the U.S. Spies on Dissent.* London, UK: Pluto Press, 2022.

Sonia Purnell. *A Woman of No Importance: The Untold Story of the American Spy Who Helped Win World War II.* New York, NY: Penguin, 2020.

Edward Snowden. *Permanent Record.* New York, NY: Picador, 2019.

Tracy Walder with Jessica Anya Blau. *The Unexpected Spy: From the CIA to the FBI, My Secret Life Taking Down Some of the World's Most Notorious Terrorists.* New York, NY: St. Martin's Griffin, 2020.

Calder Walton. *Spies: The Epic Intelligence War Between East and West.* New York, NY: Simon & Schuster, 2023.

Amy B. Zegart. *Spies, Lies, and Algorithms: The History and Future of American Intelligence.* Princeton, NJ: Princeton University Press, 2022.

Shoshana Zuboff. *The Age of Surveillance Capitalism: The Fight for a Human Future at the New Frontier of Power.* New York, NY: Public Affairs, 2019.

Index

A

Abbott, Tony, 71, 72, 75–76
Al Qaeda, 41, 122–125
artificial intelligence (AI), 24, 132–134, 136, 137, 138
Australia, 58, 59–63, 71, 72, 75–76, 145, 146–147

B

Biden, Joe, 20, 26, 27, 107, 127
bin Laden, Osama, 18, 28–29
Bush, George W., 75, 99, 110, 122, 123

C

Canada, 58, 59–63
Capitol riot on January 6, 2021, 127
Central Intelligence Agency (CIA), 18, 65, 87, 97, 110, 123
  mind-control experiments, 15, 18, 49–54
  Osama bin Laden and, 28–29
  oversight of, 40–48
  Ukraine and, 25–32
China, 20, 41, 61, 62, 77, 80, 86, 104
codes, breaking encrypted, 18
Cold War, 14, 19–24, 41, 50, 60, 85
Communism, 21, 22, 23, 50
Constitution, U.S.
Fourth Amendment, 97, 106, 109, 112, 119–120
  surveillance as violation of, 106–112, 119–120
corporations, spying on individuals, 16, 131–160
covert intelligence, 66, 67–68, 70
covert operations, 66, 68
COVID-19 pandemic, 131, 139, 140–141, 145, 151, 153

D

data, collecting, 16, 45, 67, 96–99, 107–109, 110, 111, 131, 151, 155–160
  and selling, 131–138, 155
D-Day invasion, 18, 33–39
Denmark, 58, 77–81
Department of Homeland Security, 123
diplomatic espionage, 64–70
diplomatic immunity, 64, 65, 67–70

E

employees, surveillance of, 16, 131, 139–143, 144–148, 149–154

F

far-right extremism, 126–127

Federal Bureau of Investigation (FBI), 47, 95, 98, 106–111, 116, 123, 124, 127
Federal Trade Commission (FTC), 132–138
Five Eyes alliance, 58, 59–63, 86
Foreign Intelligence Surveillance Act/Court (FISA/FISC), 75, 107–109, 110, 113–120
France, 33–39, 58, 77, 78
Fuchs, Klaus, 22

G

Germany, 14, 22, 33–39, 52–53, 58, 60, 68, 71–73, 77, 78, 81, 83, 85, 87–88, 100
Gottlieb, Sidney, 49–54
Great Britain/United Kingdom, 14, 16, 22, 33–38, 58, 59–63

H

Hitler, Adolf, 34, 36–37, 38–39
human rights issues, 18, 119

I

Indonesia, 61, 71, 72, 76
Iran, 20, 42, 47, 85–86, 87
ISIS 125–126

J

Japan, 50, 52–53, 60, 75, 86, 88

K

Kochava, 132–138

L

LSD, 50–52

M

Macron, Emmanuel, 58, 80
Manhattan Project, 19–24
Merkel, Angela, 58, 72–73, 78, 80, 83, 87, 100

N

National Security Agency (NSA), 15–16, 62, 74, 78–79, 93, 94–100, 101–105, 107, 110–111, 123
New Zealand, 58, 59–63
North Korea, 41, 47, 87
Norway, 77, 78
nuclear weapons, 15, 19–24, 41–42, 47, 65, 85

O

Obama, Barack, 27, 71–74, 95, 96, 98, 100, 124
Office of the Director of National Intelligence (ODNI), 95, 96, 97–98, 100, 107, 111
Oppenheimer, J. Robert, 19–24
opposing viewpoints, importance of, 11–13

P

Pakistan, 28–29
Patriot Act, 99, 116, 118
productivity paranoia, 145

Putin, Vladimir, 18, 20, 23, 25, 26, 29, 30, 31–32, 86

R

Russia, 34–35, 61, 77 , 80, 86, 88, 104

S

September 11, 2001, terrorist attacks, 28, 40, 41–42, 46, 76, 80, 84, 86, 93, 113, 121–123, 124
Snowden, Edward, 15–16, 62, 68, 81, 93, 94, 95–97, 100, 101–105, 108–109, 110, 111
social media, 125–126, 127, 135, 153
South Korea, 58, 74–75, 86, 87, 88
Soviet Union, 15, 19–24, 27–28, 34–35, 41, 60, 62, 85
spies, fictional, 14–15
spying
  by corporations, 16, 131–160
  history of, 14, 16
  mistakes and triumphs in, 18–54
  spying on allies, 15, 58–89, 93, 100
  spying on citizens, 15–16, 93–127, 131
surveillance capitalism, 131
Sweden, 77, 78

T

terrorism, 18, 28, 40, 41–42, 46, 47, 62, 76, 80, 84–85, 93, 110, 113, 121–127, 159
  domestic, 126–127

Trudeau, Justin, 60
Trump, Donald, 46–47
  Capitol riot, 127

U

Ukraine, 18, 20, 25–32, 77
United States and spying
  D-Day invasion, 33–39
  Five Eyes alliance, 58, 59–63, 86
  history of, 14, 16, 18
  invasion of Ukraine and, 25–32
  oversight of intelligence, 40–48, 93, 95–99
  spying on allies, 58–89, 93, 100
  spying on citizens, 15–16, 93, 94–127, 131

W

Washington, George, 14, 16
whistleblowers, 16, 93, 102, 103, 110, 153
World War II, 14, 18, 19, 22–23, 33–39, 40, 60

Index

Espionage and Intelligence